78TH ANNUAL Writer's Digest Writing Competition

COLLECTION

The Grand-Prize and First-Place
Manuscripts in Each Category of the 78th
Annual *Writer's Digest* Writing Competition

90070 • *Writer's Digest* • 4700 East Galbraith Road • Cincinnati, OH 45236

INTRODUCTION

The editors of *Writer's Digest* are pleased to share with you the winning entries in each category of the 78th Annual *Writer's Digest* Writing Competition, along with the Grand Prize-winning feature article, "Condors in a Coal Mine," by John Moir.

A special thanks goes to our esteemed panel of judges:

- Judge **Liza N. Burby** is the author of *How to Publish Your Children's Book*, 38 nonfiction children's books and one YA novel. She's also an award-winning freelance journalist. You can sign up for her children's book industry e-newsletter at lizaburby.com.

- Judge **Ann Byle** is the author of *The Making of a Christian Bestseller* and *Plainfield Township*, and co-author of *Devotions for the Soul Surfer* (with Bethany Hamilton). She's a book reviewer for *Publishers Weekly* and a freelance reporter and editor whose work has appeared in *Christian Home & School*, *Biblical Archaeological Review*, *Devozine* and more.

- Judge **James Cummins** is the author of five books of poems, most recently *Then & Now* and *Jim and Dave Defeat the Masked Man*, co-authored with David Lehman. He is the curator of the *Elliston Poetry Collection* at the University of Cincinnati, where he's also an English professor.

- Judge **Chad Gervich** is a TV producer, author of *Small Screen, Big Picture: A Writer's Guide to the TV Business* and award-winning playwright. As an executive at the Littlefield Company/Paramount Television and NBC Studios, he helped develop and maintain scripted series and pilots for ABC, NBC, CBS, FOX, UPN and the WB. He writes for *Writer's Digest*, *Variety*, *Fade In* and *Orange Coast*.

- Judge **Hollis Gillespie** is a syndicated humor columnist, NPR commentator and stand-up comedian who has appeared on *The Tonight Show with Jay Leno*. Her most recent book is *Trailer Trashed: My Dubious Efforts Toward Upward Mobility*, and her blogging workshops and book deal "boot camp" programs (hollisgillespie.com/seminars.htm) are currently on tour.

- Judge **J.A. Konrath** is the author of the Lt. "Jack" Daniels thrillers, the latest of which is *Cherry Bomb*. His books have been published in 10 languages, and he's sold more than 70 stories and articles since 2004. Visit him at jakonrath.com.

- Judge **Debby Mayne**—writer, teacher and speaker—has been an author of fiction and nonfiction for nearly 20 years. Her latest releases include *Christmas Homecoming* and *Be Still ... and Let Your Nail Polish Dry*.

- Judge **Miriam Sagan**'s newest poetry book is *Map of the Lost*. She founded and runs the creative writing program at Santa Fe Community

College. She's been a writer-in-residence at Everglades National Park, Petrified Forest National Park and THE LAND/an art site, where she's penning poetry about ecological issues.

• Judge **Julie Wheeler** is a creative writing and composition instructor for the University of Colorado at Colorado Springs. She has authored countless columns and articles on a range of high-tech topics, and she's the co-author of *Keys to Success Reader*.

• Judge **Aury Wallington** is the author of the *New York Times* bestseller *Heroes: Saving Charlie*. Her TV credits include *Sex and the City* and *Veronica Mars*. Her one-woman show *Virgin of the Vieux Carre* had a sold-out run in New York in 2003.

Finally, our most heartfelt congratulations to the winners and entrants in this year's competition. The quality of your entries makes the judging more difficult each year. We look forward to seeing your work in the 79th Annual *Writer's Digest* Writing Competition Collection.

TABLE OF CONTENTS

CONDORS IN A COAL MINE
CALIFORNIA'S LEAD BULLET BAN PROTECTS CONDORS AND OTHER WILDLIFE, BUT ITS BIGGEST BENEFICIARIES MAY BE HUMANS

John Moir
Santa Cruz, CA

It was early winter in 2005, the end of deer-hunting season in Central California, and condor biologist Joe Burnett of the Ventana Wildlife Society was steeling himself for a task he had come to dread. Burnett and a team of four Condor Recovery Program members were at a remote site in the mountains east of Big Sur, where they were trapping condors and testing them for lead poisoning.

Three team members were restraining an adult female known as Condor 208. Their arms encircled her body, and one person clamped the bird's powerful jaws shut. Burnett grabbed a syringe.

"Okay, here we go," he said. The team members tightened their hold, and Burnett plunged the needle into the bird's leg. The condor flinched.

Burnett transferred a drop of blood to a glass slide and inserted it into a portable instrument that tests blood for lead. It takes the instrument three minutes to give a reading; Burnett calls the waiting time "180 seconds from hell." An eerie silence enveloped the group as they awaited a prognosis on the bird's fate.

The machine beeped and displayed the test result: High. The bird's blood-lead level was elevated beyond the instrument's range. Condor 208 was in mortal danger.

The team rushed Condor 208 to the Los Angeles Zoo, where more sophisticated tests showed her blood-lead level to be more than ten times higher than acceptable. Veterinarians confined Condor 208 in a small pen and started twice-daily injections of a chelating agent to flush the lead from her body. It was the beginning of a desperate, round-the-clock attempt to save her life.

*   *   *

Prior to the Gold Rush, the California condor's population had remained stable for thousands of years. The birds soared on their nine-and-one-half-foot wingspans over much of the West. But beginning in the mid-1800s, a massive influx of new settlers upended the region's ecology and like so

4

many other species, the condor began to plunge toward extinction. Shooting, egg collecting, and especially poisoning decimated the bird's population. By 1982, only 22 individuals remained.

Alarmed that our nation's largest bird was on its way to becoming a museum relic, a remarkable team of scientists embarked on one of the most controversial and high-profile recovery programs in conservation history. Through a captive-breeding program, the Condor Recovery Program has succeeded in increasing the condor's total population to its current level of more than 300 birds. About 150 of these condors have been released to fly free in several Western states.

Lead poisoning was the main reason for the condor's decline, and lead remains the primary obstacle to the bird's recovery. For years, the birds have been poisoned when they consume tiny fragments of lead bullets left in hunter-shot game. Hunting season is a particularly perilous time when the number of lead poisoning incidents spikes.

Lead bullet fragments were first shown to be killing condors in 1984. As the years passed and evidence accumulated documenting the harm caused by spent ammunition, condor biologists realized that if they could not solve the lead-bullet issue, the bird's future was hopeless.

Advocates for banning lead bullets point out that alternatives—such as solid copper bullets—offer what is considered some of the best ammunition available. A simple switch to alternative ammunition would stop the dispersal of thousands of tons of lead across our landscape each year. At the same time, it would preserve the sport of hunting, which provides a significant food source for condors.

Some gun groups—including the National Rifle Association—have lobbied against any restrictions on lead ammunition. They object to the higher cost of alternative ammunition and still don't believe the research linking poisoned condors to lead bullet fragments. Many opponents view attempts to regulate lead ammunition as an attack on their right to hunt. For more than two decades, their fierce opposition prevented the enactment of legislation to curtail the use of toxic lead bullets.

Last year, in one of the most significant developments in condor conservation history, California legislators passed a bill restricting lead bullets. Despite intense lobbying by gun organizations, Governor Arnold Schwarzenegger signed the legislation that requires the use of nonlead ammunition for big game hunting in much of California beginning in July 2008.

"The lead bullet ban is a huge step forward and gives the condor a real chance for recovery," said Kelly Sorenson, executive director of the Ventana Wildlife Society. "But there are only a few game wardens to enforce this law. Its success will depend on hunters understanding that lead is deadly."

Although California's new lead bullet ban will protect condors and other wildlife, intriguing new research suggests that the biggest beneficiaries may be *humans*.

* * *

In 2007, the condor's lead poisoning problems caught the attention of William Cornatzer, a physician in Bismarck, North Dakota, who had joined the Board of Directors for the Peregrine Fund, the group that manages condor releases near the Grand Canyon.

An avid hunter, Cornatzer was intrigued by studies demonstrating what happens to a lead bullet when it hits a game animal. Condor biologists had shown that the bullet shatters into dozens and sometimes hundreds of tiny fragments that scatter widely from the wound site, leaving behind a deadly "snowstorm" of toxic lead that poisons condors and other scavengers such as ravens and bald eagles. Audubon California has identified 48 birds and animals that are harmed by spent ammunition. *I wonder*, Cornatzer thought, *if humans might also be at risk.*

Early in 2008, Cornatzer contacted the North Dakota Department of Health and arranged to collect 100 one-pound packages of ground venison donated by hunters to North Dakota food pantries. A radiologist helped Cornatzer run CT scans on the packages. They were stunned to discover that 59 of them contained metal fragments.

"The scans just lit up with tiny bits of metal," Cornatzer said. "I almost fell over. I could not believe how much metal was in the meat."

The North Dakota Department of Health ran additional scans that showed the metal fragments tested strongly for lead. Concerned about the potential risks for humans, North Dakota officials recommended the destruction of tons of venison still in storage at food pantries.

Spurred by the North Dakota findings, health departments in several other states ran similar tests and also found tainted meat. In the largest survey of donated venison, Minnesota officials X-rayed 1,239 packages and found 22 percent contaminated with lead.

"The lead fragments are so small that you can't feel them in your mouth when you are eating venison burgers or sausage," Cornatzer said.

Because of the possible consequences for humans, North Dakota's Department of Health and the Centers for Disease Control and Prevention (CDC) are currently analyzing the blood-lead levels of 740 North Dakotans. The study participants were asked about possible sources of lead exposure—including game. The complete results are expected sometime next year. Chinaro Kennedy, a CDC epidemiologist leading the study, says, "the number one thing people need to be aware of is the potential risk from lead—even in small doses."

The symptoms of low-level lead poisoning are insidious, ranging from hearing loss and high blood pressure to cardiovascular disease, stroke, and kidney damage. Young children exposed to lead can suffer permanent intellectual impairment. In 2006, research conducted at Tulane University showed that blood-lead levels that were once thought safe are linked to a higher risk of death from a range of causes.

In May 2008, the Peregrine Fund sponsored a conference that brought together for the first time wildlife biologists and human health experts to examine the implications of ingesting spent lead ammunition.

"The overwhelming message from the conference was that people just haven't thought about the possibility that lead bullet fragments could be a source of sub-lethal human poisoning," said Rick Watson, vice president of the Peregrine Fund.

Calls have already begun for a nationwide ban on lead ammunition. The Humane Society of the United States, as well as a 2008 California Condor Blue Ribbon Panel sponsored by the American Ornithologists' Union and Audubon California, have recommended that hunters *everywhere* switch to alternative ammunition.

* * *

Condor 208 barely survived her massive lead poisoning. After she endured five stressful weeks of rehabilitation at the Los Angeles Zoo, veterinarians released her back into the chaparral-covered mountains near Big Sur. In the spring of 2007, Condor 208 and a mate nested in a remote sandstone cliff, and she gave birth to the first condor chick born in Central California in more than 100 years. The baby condor was named Centennia.

Since the ban on lead ammunition is so new, Joe Burnett still has to test condors for lead poisoning. But Burnett is hopeful that someday he can dispense with his syringe and field blood lab. For the first time in decades, the condor's prospects look brighter.

Additional research will be needed to investigate more fully the potential human health risks of ingesting lead from hunter-shot game. In the meantime, across the country most hunters continue to use lead bullets to shoot the game they bring home for their families to eat. Many of them are unaware of the hidden danger that could lurk in their meat.

Like canaries in a coal mine, the condors are acting as sentinels, providing a warning for anyone eating hunter-shot game. This ancient bird is telling us to pay attention—and to be careful.

—end—

A BOWL OF RICE

Barbara Chamberlain
Aptos, CA

Long ago, on the island of Okinawa

Kiyoshi's stomach growled as he chopped a head of cabbage for Mitsu, the cook.

"Thank you, Kiyoshi," she said, filling bowl with steaming rice.

"You are most welcome," he answered, swallowing hard, his body shaking as he fought back gnawing hunger.

He bowed slightly, "Do you think there is a chance for me to become a houseboy here soon?"

"If one of the houseboys leaves, I'll send for you. I promise." She smiled kindly. "Go now before my master returns."

Running out of the house, he imagined the Kara-shi-shi, the stone lion on the roof by the door to frighten away evil spirits, leered at him. Kiyoshi dashed down the road clutching the bowl of rice like a cup of gold until he turned on the path that led to his lonely cave in the forest.

Kiyoshi hated the idea of begging. He wanted a home and a job, but no household needed him. He combed the beach for driftwood, shellfish, and often caught fish in his homemade net. When hunger began to defeat him he could always depend on the kind Mitsu. The smell of the warm rice in the bowl made his nose quiver. He sat on a rock by the side of the road, shoveling the sticky rice into his mouth.

He had always been alone. Did some poor family abandon him or did he wander into the forest and become lost? His saddest thought was that he would never know.

I must save some of this for tomorrow, he told himself, forcing his fingers to take only a few grains of rice at a time.

He looked up, surprised to see an old Tanme (grandfather) walking unsteadily along the path. His long beard stood out against a faded kimono. He smiled brightly when he saw Kiyoshi.

Leaning on his cane he asked, "Young man, is there a house nearby?"

Kiyoshi nodded and pointed down the road. Slowly he realized that the old man's blue veined hands were trembling. The grandfather wiped his wrinkled face with a cloth and sank to the ground, as though he had reached the end of his long life's journey.

"What is it?" Kiyoshi cried. "May I help you, grandfather? Where is your

8

family? You are too old to be out on the road by yourself."

"I have no family." His tired, brown eyes reflected a sadness that Kiyoshi recognized. "They are all gone. My sons and their wives went out to fish the morning of a sudden typhoon. The demon wind took them."

This was a tragedy for an ancient one to have no family to give him a home.

"Are you hungry, grandfather?"

"Yes," A rasping sigh answered.

Kiyoshi gulped, handing his bowl to the man. "Please take some of my rice."

He swallowed hard with each scoop the grandfather ate.

The old man cleaned the bowl. "You have saved my life. Will your mother give you more?"

Kiyoshi, his eyes fixed on the bamboo design in his barren bowl, answered. "I have no mother or parents, Tanme. There is no more. I worked at a house for that rice. If you want shelter in my cave I will try to net some fish for us in the morning."

Under his wide-brimmed straw hat, an odd glint sparkled in his dark eyes. His forehead wrinkled. "Forgive old Mabuni. Why else would you be eating out on the road. You have no family?"

"No. You may share my cave tonight," Kiyoshi offered.

Tanme always knew many wonderful stories and they carried the wisdom of a lifetime in their minds.

Kiyoshi had often wished for such a man as a teacher.

"I can go no farther, Kiyoshi. I shall accept your kind offer, only for tonight."

Kiyoshi helped him to his feet. With each step the old man's walking stick made a distinctive hole in the grass. He admired the finely carved cane, an inheritance from the grandfather's happier days.

Mabuni asked, "You do not fear the jungle?"

"I know almost every blade of grass. You are afraid because you do not."

"You are wise for one so young."

Inside the cave were the possessions gleaned from the beach-a rusty lantern, a few candles, an iron cooking pot, three blankets and mats Kiyoshi wove from tall grass.

Mabuni gasped when he saw a huge spider as large as a man's chest resting quietly in his web that covered the top of the cave.

"Kiyoshi, how can you live with that creature?"

"I moved in with him," Kiyoshi explained. "He helps me by eating flies and mosquitoes. He does not bother people."

Mabuni gulped. A mongoose dashed into the cave entrance and as quickly disappeared into the green bush.

"He is my friend, too," Kiyoshi explained. "He kills the snakes."

Mabuni sank to a tattered straw mat. "You have realized that nature can be used to your advantage."

"To be honest, I had no choice." The boy sank to another mat. "Grandfather, will you tell me a story?"

"Close your eyes, Kiyoshi, and I will tell you abut the great turtle that carries Okinawa on its back in the China Sea."

Even though Kiyoshi knew there was no such turtle, the old Tanme wove a superb story that kept Kyoshi's mind whirling until he fell asleep. For the first time he dreamt pleasant dreams, listening to the old grandfather's tales while Kiyoshi showed the old man his world. He would no longer be alone in the dark cave.

Kiyoshi woke to the singing birds of morning. "Grandfather, I can make tea," he began. The rest of the words died in echoes that gradually faded in the cave.

The mat was empty.

Maybe he was a dream.

"No, why would I roll out another mat?" Kiyoshi asked the black spider. The morning sun rays outlined the web. Some of the strands were broken. Since he always avoided the fine web, Kiyoshi knew that the old man had broken them.

Maybe he just went outside.

Kiyoshi searched. The old grandfather was gone and so were Kiyoshi's hopes.

He finally came back to the cave, his throat sore from calling, his eyes burning with tears. He fought the tears and lost, sobbing until he could cry no more.

The shadow of the spider jumped from one wall of the cave to the other. The creature pounced on his prey, a large, unlucky beetle.

The sad spectacle of nature made Kiyoshi realize that he was hungry. He had no desire to eat the large beetles.

"I'll make some tea and then go to the beach." When he opened his jar of homemade tea, something in the corner of the cave caught his eye.

The poor grandfather's cane was leaning in a quiet corner.

"The old man must have meant to return. He could barely walk!"

Kiyoshi's fingers lifted the cane. He ran his fingers over the carvings of shells, the moon, the sun, and the stars. The cane felt warm and comforting, almost as though it were alive. "Tell me, where is your master?" To Kiyoshi's shock, the cane whirled in his hands, struck the dirt once, twice, three times, bouncing back to the spot where it had been left. Frightened, the boy stared at it.

His arms felt cold in the damp cave. He ran outside to the warm sun. Gasping, the boy sank down to a large gray rock that often served as his dinner table. A strange sound filled the air behind him. *Tap….tap…tap.*

Kiyoshi turned his head slowly. His throat felt paralyzed He wanted to scream but could not. His eyes widened.

The cane followed him out of the cave!

It bounced to the rock and leaned against his trembling hand.

Unable to move, the boy prayed for help.

His mind slowly became aware of more noises in the forest. The ground trembled with the sound vibrations made only by the hooves of horses.

Four soldiers mounted on horses entered the clearing. They wore swords.

Kiyoshi wanted to hide.

"You! Young man with the cane!" One shouted.

Kiyoshi managed a croaking whisper. "It is not my cane. It belonged to a grandfather would has disappeared. I looked for him. Sirs, I did not steal it."

In his fear he sank to his knees.

One of the men dismounted. "I know. Look up, Kiyoshi."

The boy forced his eyes up to look at the man. He was Mabuni.

Again Kiyoshi's voice failed him.

The man reached down to help him stand. "What is happening?"

"Your majesty," one of the soldiers said. "Do you want the boy on your horse?"

"Yes, but give me a minute to explain to him."

"Certainly, your majesty."

The soldier explained, "This is your King Mabini, ruler of Okinawa and the Ryuku Islands. You have received a great honor."

"Kiyoshi," the king began, "I told you the truth about my sons. They are dead. There has been no heir to my throne for five years. It was time for the cane to choose a new ruler for these lands. The nobles thrust their sons at me. They are spoiled sons of the upper class. Most of them think of themselves, of their clothes, of their own comforts."

The boy could do nothing except to stare, first at the king and then at the cane.

"I was chosen to be king by the cane of the ancients. After two years of fruitless searching for an heir, I decided to go on a journey among my people."

"Why didn't you say who you were?"

"People treat kings graciously. They flatter and try to gain favors. Beggers in rags do not get quite the same treatment. Some people are kind enough to give food. Many shoved me away. The cane, though, kept me going. It found you. You are kind and shared with me everything you had. You know from your difficult life how to cope with an often not-so-kind world."

"May I be a houseboy in your palace?" Kiyoshi asked.

The king chuckled. "You will come to live with me. You will learn and someday, you will be king of these islands."

At first Kiyoshi did not understand what was happening to him. He worked hard.

Since he knew what it was like to be the poorest of the poor, the man he became understood the people more than any other ruler. Sometimes he and the cane would disappear "to speak to a spider." The new king built a shrine by the cave in the forest.

He never wanted to forget his origins that made him the greatest island king.

ALTERNATIVE TREATMENTS FOR AUTISM

Renee Roberson
Huntersville, NC

Actress and autism advocate Jenny McCarthy brought biomedical treatments for autism to the forefront a few years ago, when she shared her son's story with the world. Today, she serves as a board member and spokesperson for Generation Rescue, a parent-founded and parent-led organization focused on biomedical treatment for autism.

Where autism was once considered a strictly neurological disorder, researchers now are discovering clues that point to problems arising from inflammation in the immune system and gut, according to Judy Converse, a licensed registered dietitian who specializes in pediatric nutrition and the author of "Special Needs Kids Eat Right: Strategies to Help Kids on the Autism Spectrum Focus, Learn and Thrive" (Penguin, 2009). Many children with autism share the same physical symptoms, including gastrointestinal distress, food allergies, immune issues, vitamin and mineral deficiencies and sleep disturbances.

"I sought out biomedical treatment for William when I talked to another mom who saw big changes in her son from the Gluten-Free/Casein-Free Diet (GFCF), and I know she found out from another mom," says Charlotte mom Lindsay Kluttz.

"There is so much that doctors can't tell us because they just don't know at this point in time," she says. "Unfortunately, we can't wait for peer-reviewed science to confirm what moms and a certain few specialists already know because it will be too late to help."

What is Autism?

Autism is a complex neurobiological disorder that typically lasts throughout a person's lifetime. It is part of a group of disorders known as autism spectrum disorders (ASDs). Symptoms can be very mild or severe. According to the latest information provided by the Centers for Disease Control, 1 in 150 children in the United States are diagnosed with autism.

It occurs in all races and socioeconomic groups, and is four times more likely to strike boys than girls, with 1 in 94 boys receiving an autism diagnosis. Autism impairs a person's ability to communicate and relate to others. It also is associated with rigid routines and repetitive behaviors, such as obsessively arranging objects. While there is no clear cut cause for the prevalence of autism in our society today, many advocates and activists believe it is a combination of genetic predisposition; the overuse of antibiotics; the prevalence of heavy metals, like mercury, in our air, water and food; and the increase in vaccines children receive today.

For example, in the 1980s, the recommended vaccine schedule included 10 shots by age 6. Today it is 36. Experts at the Centers for Disease control agree there are more children than ever currently being diagnosed with autism, but say that it is unclear how much of this increase is due to changes in how we identify and classify ASDs in children, and how much is due to a true increase in prevalence.

"There are a bunch of tools that have to click together like a puzzle," says Converse. "If you leave one out, it's only as good as it's weakest piece."

Dr. Kenneth Haas, a chiropractor and registered DAN! physician with Haas Wellness Centers in Charlotte, notes there is an overwhelming amount of information that can be found in books, chat rooms and online about the best way to treat autism. Because of this, he says parents should not attempt to put together their own treatment plan without first consulting a trusted physician.

"Parents need a coach on what to do first," he advises.

The DAN! (Defeat Autism Now) Protocol

Claims over the various causes of ASDs obviously have proven to be controversial and have sparked debate among medical professionals and parents looking for answers. In the past, parents receiving a diagnosis of autism for their child simply were told to accept it as part of their lives and recommended to begin applied behavioral analysis therapies, which teach children with autism specific social behaviors with a rewards and consequences system.

But in recent years, a group of doctors called DAN! doctors have come on the scene, focusing on treating autism with detoxification, nutritional supplements, special diets, treatment of intestinal inflammation and chelation, or the removal of heavy metals from the body intravenously or with medication, which can be potentially dangerous if not administered correctly.

Currently, there are at least 400 doctors in the United States dedicated to treating children with autism biomedically, including Haas, who believes early intervention is critical in cases of autism.

"Time is definitely your enemy when it comes to neurological disorders," he says.

Diet and Healing the Gut

Children with autism have difficulty absorbing wheat and dairy foods, are often constipated and, essentially, feel as if they are under the effect of opiates, explains Converse.

"We can talk about recovery from any disease, why not autism?" she says, noting she has seen many children in her practice move up the autism spectrum and even lose their diagnosis completely.

Charlotte mom Chelsea Mellon started her son on the GFCF diet last August and added a variety of supplements and probiotics to his daily routine. She says she has seen tremendous progress in her son, who is on the high end of the spectrum and taught himself to read by age 3 1/2.

Mellon says her son's childhood gastrointestinal issues were resolved within just a few weeks, his speech improved drastically, and he is now a very verbal and personable child. "Compared to a year ago, my son is excelling," she says.

Converse, who runs a private practice in Colorado, has met many young patients who were repeatedly exposed to antibiotics as infants, and their intestinal tracts were never replenished with a supply of the necessary good bacteria. In her book, she discusses how the first two years of life are a "critical window for acquiring the necessary helpful bacteria in a baby's intestine." The wrong balance can cause holes in the intestine (also known as "leaky gut" syndrome), food allergies or intolerances, constipation, irritable stools, frequent illness and can interfere with growth. Therefore, healing the gut and working to maintain a proper intestinal balance with a combination of probiotics and proper nutritional care is one of the first steps on the road to treating autism biomedically.

Putting the Pieces Together

More often than not, children with autism also have an overgrowth of yeast in their intestinal tracts from antibiotic use, says Haas. This is where antifungals come into play. Haas only recommends natural antifungal remedies, such as garlic and caprylic acid, but other physicians may prescribe stronger medications for their patients.

Kluttz says she tried the GFCF diet at first with her son, as well as weeded out foods that triggered allergies. But she saw the most improvement a few days after he began taking the antifungal medication Diflucan.

"He absolutely still has autism," Kluttz says. "But I'm witnessing that every day he moves closer to recovering from it. ... Even if that day never officially comes, I'm eternally grateful for the functioning he's gained."

For many parents, the hardest part is piecing the puzzle together, as what works for one child may not work for another. Converse says that while seeing patients achieve success, she has also seen autistic patients throughout the course of her practice who have not responded to these types of treatments at all.

The American Academy of Pediatrics directs physicians to encourage patients and family members to educate themselves about alternative health options, but many medical professionals dismiss the merits of anything outside conventional medical treatments.

Regarding complementary and alternative medicine treatments for autism, the following precautionary statements can be found on the Web site for the Centers for Disease Control:

"These types of treatments are very controversial. Current research shows that as many as one third of children with autism may have tried complementary or alternative medicine treatments, and up to 10 percent may be using a potentially dangerous treatment. Before starting such a treatment, check it out carefully, and talk to your child's health care professional.

If you are thinking about changing your child's diet, talk to his or her health care professional first. Or talk with a nutritionist to be sure your child is getting the essential nutrients he or she needs."

Whatever course of treatment parents seek for their child, most say the support of other parents is essential. For a list of local support groups in the Charlotte area, visit the "community" section of www.autismspeaks.org. CMC-Northeast also hosts an autism support group the fourth Thursday of each month from 6:30 p.m. to 7:30 p.m. For more information, call 704-403-2660.

What are some of the signs of autism?
A child with autism might:
• not play "pretend" games (like pretending to feed a doll)
• not point at objects to show interest
• avoid eye contact and want to be alone
• prefer not to be held or cuddled, or might cuddle only when he or she wants to
• avoid social interaction
• repeat or echo words or phrases he or she hears, or repeat words or phrases in place of normal language (echoalia)
• have trouble expressing needs using typical words or motions
• repeat actions over and over again
• have trouble adapting when a routine changes
• have unusual reactions to smells, tastes, sights, sounds, or textures
• lose skills (liking not saying certain words)
Source: Centers for Disease Control

Autism Fast Facts
• 1 in 150 children are diagnosed with autism
• 1 in 94 boys receive an autism diagnosis
• 67 children are diagnosed every day
• A new case is diagnosed every 20 minutes
• Autism receives less than 5 percent of the research funding of many less prevalent childhood diseases.
Source: Autism Speaks

FRONTIER JUSTICE

Mart Shaughnessy
Perris, CA

Rod Gantry felt the full weight of his fifty-eight years as he ambled through the mesquite, deep in the Canelo Hills. Hot, tired, irritable and alone, he'd spent the last twelve days in pursuit of a cougar that had seemed intent on leading him over every hill and through every canyon in southern Arizona.

When he heard the thunder from the Harley-Davidson engines, Junior, his three year old appaloosa stallion began to fret and crow hop. Rod pulled up and stroked the horse's mane.

"Easy boy, it's just a bunch of bikers. Let's wander south a ways and cross the road down by that wash."

Rod had spent a life-time riding the desert trails. And he'd often enjoyed an evening campfire with a family or group of motorcycle and ATV enthusiasts. He had found them to be as appreciative of natures gifts as he was. But, this group appeared to be cut from a little rougher bark than those.

As he began to veer away, they spotted him and maneuvered their bikes intercepting him at the wash. "Hey, Dad, who do you think you are, John Wayne?"

Rod glared at the man.

"Hey, Pops! I'm talkin' to you. What're you all dressed up for, some kinda Halloween deal?"

Rod, was dressed like a character out of an old B-Western. And he probably could've had a few laughs with these folks if he thought they were just funnin' with him.

But Rod Gantry had a keen sense for reading people. And as he sat squinting into the sun, his gaze darting from face to face, sizing up this crowd they didn't look to be what he'd call, solid citizens. He eased out of the saddle, removed his hat, looped the stampede string over the horn, turned and stepped toward the man he perceived to be the leader.

The biker had a thick dark beard and long hair that fell in ringlets across his shoulders. He stood a good six-foot-three and looked to dress-out at about two-fifty. A thick neck and chest were parenthesized by huge, tattoo covered arms. Sharp, beady eyes glowered from deep beneath a Neanderthal forehead.

He shut down the Harley, slid out of the saddle and swaggered to where

17

Rod stood. The big man pounded a ham-hock fist into his open hand and squinted menacingly at Rod. He spoke over his shoulder in a sing-song voice an octave too high, "Hey, fellas, look at this. Old Pops here thinks he's tough. I do believe he wants to try me."

"Me," was the last word the biker would speak through a full set of his own teeth. He sucked in air, his eyes rounded and he stood frozen in place as a huge right hand crashed into his jaw and snapped his head back. His knees buckled and as he began to fall, Rod hooked him with a left shattering his cheekbone and smashing his nose against the side of his face. Blood flew from his mouth and nose and his buddies caught him as he fell.

With his pals holding him upright the biker was an easy target. And Rod followed up the first right-left combination with a set of straight shots, pulping the big man's nose and lips.

"Jesus Christ, mister!" Someone murmured as the bloody biker slid to the ground.

Rod stood alert, fists clenched, eyes glaring. Fifteen hard cases returned his stare. Sound ceased to exist and the silence pounded in his head.

"I know what you're thinking", he said. "And you can probably get it done. But before you do several of you are gonna bleed. And, you're gonna have to kill me to stop me. Now what you have to ask yourself is this. Is it worth it? Is it worth all that effort for one old fart like me?"

He nodded toward their leader. "You'd be better off takin' the time to get your friend to a doctor."

Then he turned, stepped into the saddle, screwed his hat down tight and weaved Junior through the crowd.

A young girl stepped forward and looked up at him. "Mister, you sure have a pretty horse."

Rod checked the appy back. "Thanks, I'm partial to him."

"Mister would you take me out of here? I don't like these people. I could make it well worth your trouble." She ran her tongue across her lips and smiled.

He glanced over his shoulder at the sullen crowd. "I guess I could take you back to Patagonia, if Junior don't mind us ridin' double." He patted the stallion on the rump. "He's still a youngster and he might decide three's a crowd." Rod paused, bit his lip and shook his head. "As for making it worth my while? Missy, I'm too old and too tired, but thanks for the thought."

As they dropped down into Redrock Canyon, and turned toward Patagonia. The girl asked, "Mister, what's your name?"

"Rod, Rod Gantry."

"I'm Sonni Templeton. Sonni with an 'i'."

"Nice to meet you Sonni with an 'i'."

"Rod Gantry, are you a real cowboy?"

He pondered the question. He could have taken it as a wise crack or a taunt, but she hadn't asked in that manner.

"Let's see, am I a cowboy?" He slapped the reins against his thigh. "Well,

I guess that depends on what you mean by cowboy. If you're askin' me do I earn a livin' by watchin' the south ends of a bunch of north bound steers, the answer is no. But to me, being a cowboy is a state of mind, not an occupation."

Rod paused a moment gathering his thoughts. "A cowboy tries to do what's right, loves the outdoors and horses and dogs."

He reached up and scratched Junior between the ears. "A cowboy's true to his word and stands up for folks that can't stand up for themselves. Once a cowboy commits to somethin', he sees it through."

"And when he says until death do us part, he means it."

"Now, if that's what you mean by cowboy? Then I guess, I'm, a cowboy."

They rode on in silence for a bit. "I know all that probably sounds kinda corny to you, but that's me. My Sara used to say I was born in the wrong century."

"Is Sara your wife?"

Rod tensed and pursed his lips. "Was. My Sara was killed three years ago."

"I'm sorry. I didn't know…"

His posture softened. "That's all right, it wasn't your fault." He pushed his hat back on his head and closed his eyes. It was my fault. She went out alone at dusk. I shoulda been with her.

Soni said, "Do you mind if I ask? I mean, you said she was killed. What happened?"

"She was attacked by a mountain lion."

"Oh… That's why you're out here. You're looking for the lion."

Rod reset his hat. "You're pretty savvy for a city girl. The lion returned to our range a couple weeks ago and killed some cattle. I know it's the same cat 'cause he has five toes on his right front foot"

They picked their way through the canyon and the sun disappeared behind the Santa Ritas. With sunset came the cool evening air and Rod felt the young girl behind him shivering.

"Let's stop for a minute. You can slip into this duster, it'll keep the chill off."

Rod whoa'd Junior and helped Sonni down. Then he swung out of the saddle and handed her the white canvas coat.

As she accepted the coat he took a good look at her for the first time. She appeared to be in her early twenties, stood about five foot six, with long, auburn hair and holly green eyes. She wore shorts that highlighted long legs, a halter top that she filled to the overflow mark, and a well worn straw cowboy hat.

"Whatcha lookin' at? Thinking of taking me up on my offer?" She stared unblinking into his eyes.

"What, uh no, uh, I mean. Oh hell let's get goin'. Wait a minute." He unpacked a pair of beat up shotgun chaps. "Put these on. You're gonna chafe them bare legs raw, ridin' back there, with nothin' to protect you."

She thanked him and slipped into the duster and chaps.

As they rode on she put her arms around his waist and pulled herself close.

Finally she said. "You don't think much of me, do you?"

"Beg your pardon."

"I said you don't think much of me."

Rod took a deep breath and exhaled slowly. "If you want people to like you for who you are, you need to start likin' yourself."

"What do you mean? I like myself just fine. What's not to like? Just look at me." She sat up tall, arched her back and held her arms out.

"No, you don't." He spat back. "Don't be makin' light of this. Face up to what's real. If you did you wouldn't be offering your body to some old coot, just 'cause he's willing to give you a ride to some outta the way town in the middle of nowhere. Most anybody with an ounce of decency woulda been glad to help you. You don't have to be givin' it away to make people like you."

Rod clenched his teeth. "There, I'm sorry if I hurt your feelings, but I had to say it. I can't stand to see young people waste their lives and that's what you're doing. Take a good look at yourself and tell me I'm wrong."

He felt her sobbing as they rode on in silence.

Finally they topped out on a rise and could see the lights of Patagonia. He felt her swallow hard.

"You're right," she said. "I didn't like what I'd become, and over the past couple of months I'd hated it more and more. I'd made up my mind to get out but I couldn't get away."

Rod balled his fist and turned in the saddle. "You mean they been holdin' you prisoner?"

"No, no nothing like that. I wanted to leave but I was afraid of being alone."

She took in a breath and held it. "I didn't know where to go and, even if I did, I had no way to get there. I don't know if you'll understand this. I don't know if I understand it myself, but when you gave Curley that beating it gave me strength. I made up my mind I was leaving today and if you wouldn't take me I'd walk out."

She reached up and hung onto his shoulders. "I don't know where I'm going. I just know it's away from this life while I've still got a sliver of self-respect."

Rod crossed his wrists on the saddle horn. "What about home? Why don't you go home? Start over. Ain't many people get a chance to do that—or have the backbone to try. You could do it."

"You know" she said, "I haven't talked to my folks in three years. I left Sacramento when I was nineteen."

She shuddered and buried her face in his back for a moment. "I was running with a pretty rough crowd. My folks and I had a big fight about it. I told them I could pick my own friends, make my own decisions. Then I got on the back of a guy's motorcycle and we headed for Arizona."

Again she sobbed and held him tight but not like before. This was grief not seduction.

"My folks don't know where I am and I don't think they care. I can't say I blame them."

They rode quiet for a while. Rod slid his feet out of the stirrups and stretched his legs. "I'd be willing to bet they care. Call them," he said.

"Do you really think they'd let me come back home?"

"There's only one way you'll ever know. Tell them you love them. Tell 'em you want to come home."

It was early evening when Rod and Sonni rode into Patagonia. The little town housed the usual ranch supply businesses along with several antique shops, a motel, that had seen better days, and a tavern/restaurant. A boardwalk ran along the front of the shops and hitching rails gave the place the appearance of an old western town. The town was well lighted and a number of locals and tourists window shopped and visited along the store-fronts.

Rod walked the appaloosa up to the tavern. Sonni braced herself on his arm, swung down, pulled a pink cell phone from her purse and flipped it open. "Wouldn't you know it I've got zero bars."

"I don't doubt it," Rod said. "Nestled down between these hills the signal's probably bouncing all over the place."

He swung off and tied his horse next to four others snoozing, three legged, at the rail. "Let's go inside maybe they have a phone you can use."

They entered the Dew Drop Inn brushing trail dust off their clothes. The bartender looked up and smiled. "Howdy, folks, what'll it be."

Rod returned the man's smile. "We'd be obliged to use your phone and have a look at the bus schedule. The young lady's had a time of it and we need to get her on her way to Tucson."

"The pay phone's over there on the wall next to the front window, but you'll have to wait until morning for the bus. You can put up at the motel." He pointed across the street. "It's old but the rooms are clean."

Sonni went to call her parents. Rod picked a stool at the end of the bar and ordered a tall Sam Adams. He sipped his brew and appraised the eclectic decor of the Dew Drop Inn. Memorabilia hung haphazardly from the walls and ceiling: a tricycle, a Flexible-Flyer sled, a couple of milk cans and a Louisville Slugger.

Bits and pieces of Sonni's conversation filtered in and out of his consciousness as she re-connected with her parents.

…"That's right daddy I want to come home. I've missed you and mama too…."

As Rod, sat covertly listening to the girl four Harley Davidson 'Hogs' roared off the highway and skidded to a stop out front.

"Sonni," he stepped off the bar stool and strolled over to the window. "Those friends of yours back in the canyon. Any of them have a cell phone?"

"Just a minute, daddy. Yeah. Why do you ask?"

"I think somebody reached out and touched someone, and they've come here to, touch us, so to speak."

He watched the four men kick-stand their bikes and start toward the tavern. One of the men had a police baton, one carried a tire iron, another had a switchblade, and the fourth slowly flicked a piece of chain about eighteen inches long.

<u>Interesting,</u> Rod thought, <u>no guns.</u> <u>Looks like they've got a good old fashioned beatin' in mind.</u> He reached up and took the Louisville Slugger from the wall. It was a kid's bat, about twenty-eight inches long, not the size bat you'd choose to try to hit one out of Wrigley Field, but perfect for what he had in mind. Striding for the door he smiled at the bartender.

"Don't worry, I'll bring it right back."

Gravel crunched beneath his feet as he jogged into the parking area. He stopped next to a Ford Caravan, turned and faced the four assailants.

As they closed in, threatening with their weapons, one of them called to Rod. "I'm Rocky, this here's Burt, Craig, and Harlan."

"That supposed to mean something to me?" Rod answered wrist- flipping the bat in his left hand.

"Just thought you might want to know the names of the guys who're gonna leave you wishing you were dead." The four men stopped, forming a semi-circle about fifteen feet from their prey.

Sonni bolted from the tavern. "Rod," she screamed. "Please! You don't need to do this."

Rocky smiled, "Tell you what old man, when we finish with you, we're gonna take your little friend and party all night.

He blew a kiss toward Sonni. "Hey sweetie you just wait. Ol' Rocky's gonna show you what it's like with a real man."

"Sonni," Rod said, remaining focused on his assailants. "You just take a chair on the porch. This ain't all that much of a handful. These boys are about two shy of what they need to get the job done."

Rod shoved the fat end of the bat into Harlan's gut. Wind gushed out like air from a slashed tire.

Then he stepped to the left and swung with one hand connecting with Burt's knee.

Burt went down screaming.

Craig, crouched like knife fighters do in the movies. He bobbed and weaved and made little circles in the air with the switchblade. Rod took a Barry Bonds grip and swung crushing the man's left arm and several ribs.

Craig moaned, dropped the knife, fell to the ground and assumed the fetal position.

Rocky drove in hard from the right, and Rod splattered his nose with a straight thrust of the bat handle.

Rocky sunk to his knees.

Harlan recovered from the first blow and came in swinging the chain over his head. "You're goin' down, chump."

Harlan had neglected to consider two important details, eighteen inch chain, twenty-eight inch bat. Rod took a full swing. The Louisville Slugger caught some of the chain and when it smacked Harlan's head, it sounded like an aluminum bat taking on a Nolan Ryan fast ball.

Harlan dropped like a rag-doll.

Staggering to his feet, Rocky stood wobbly-kneed facing Rod. Rod walked over to him patting his right hand with the meaty part of the bat.

"Well, Rocky, that leaves you and me. What was it you were gonna do to that little girl, party all night? Show her what it's like with a real man? Well, let's see what we can do to discourage that kind of thinking."

Rod swung the Slugger under-hand hitting Rocky directly between the legs. There was a sickening 'thwack,' like a two by four hitting a heavy punching bag, Rocky doubled over. But before the thug fell Rod flicked the bat around, swung the handle like an uppercut and caught him across the bridge of the nose. The gathering crowd gasped at the sound of bone and cartilage popping as blood exploded from Rocky's mouth, nose and cheeks.

Rod walked over to Burt. He could see by the position of the leg, it'd be a long, long time before the man walked without a limp.

He picked up the tire iron and Burt turned away. "No more man, I'm out of it."

With the iron securely in his left hand and the bat in his right, Rod stomped back to where Rocky lay sprawled in the dirt. "No, man, I'm finished."

A good sized crowd stood, staring, wide-eyed and gap-jawed. Rod shook his head and glared at them. Adrenalin flew through his brain, his lungs pumped as his breath came in short gasps. Then, as his focus began to expand, comments from the crowd turned from a low pitched buzz to words.

"Oh my God, did you see that?"

"A baseball bat. He beat 'em with a kids ball bat."

"What's he gonna do with that tire iron?"

"Are they all dead?"

"I don't know. But if they ain't, they're wishin' they was."

"I'll call the paramedics."

"Shouldn't we call the police?"

"Look at him, those eyes, he looks like a predator."

"Well, after what I just seen, he ain't prey, that's for damn sure."

Regaining his composure, Rod's glare softened and he dropped the tire iron. "Right now you folks are trying to decide how you feel about what just happened. You're trying to decide if I'm a hero or an animal. Well, I didn't come huntin' this. They came for me, for me and that young lady." He pointed toward the porch.

"I'd bet you all a month's pay this ain't their first rodeo. Only this time they tried to saddle the wrong bronc."

He paused and the glare returned. "I don't back up and I don't take prisoners."

Again he seemed to soften. He looked over at Sonni and winked. "I seem to have worked up an appetite," he said. And they walked back into the Dew Drop Inn.

The crowd inside greeted them with cheers as Rod handed the Louisville Slugger to the bartender.

"Here you go, just like I said, good as new."

The man took the bat, started to wiped it clean, thought better of it and displayed it, as is, above the mirror in the middle of the bar.

"You two sit at this booth right here and order anything on the menu." He said wiping the table clean. "Dinner's on the Dew Drop Inn."

Rod and Sonni were enjoying rib-eye steaks when the police officer entered the Tavern. The bartender pointed toward them and the policeman approached their table.

"Evening folks, I'm Officer Tom Nunez."

"Please sir." He said, extending his hand like a traffic cop. "Wait until you hear me out. There was an altercation in the parking lot this evening." He stopped and weighed his words. "Apparently an elderly gentleman took a baseball bat to four men. It's my understanding that he was protecting himself from these four…." He paused searching for the word. "Victims. However, the condition of the, victims makes it appear as though things went way beyond self defense. When I find the man I'll have to charge him with criminal assault."

Rod started to speak, but the officer again held up his hand.

"Please sir. We've had a series of muggings, rapes and robberies in this area. The crimes coincide with the arrival of the four victims. We've arrested them several times but could never get a conviction. Somehow, I think the crime rate around here is gonna drop."

Tom Nunez removed his pad and pencil from his shirt pocket. "Now I'm gonna go out to the parking lot and question the folks that witnessed the fight. I doubt that I'll be able to find the man they describe. If he was smart he'd probably just ride out of here."

He stopped and tapped the pencil against the pad. "I guess my report will say, some old cowboy rode out of the hills and gave these boys a taste of old fashioned frontier justice."

Then Officer Nunez, turned and marched back outside.

"Well," Rod removed his napkin. "It 'pears as though the sheriff just asked me to get outta town. Sonni, are you 'going to be all right?"

"Excuse me," interrupted the bartender extending his right hand. "My name is Carlos Bustamonte. Mister, you don't have to worry about the lady. We'll make sure she gets back to Tucson and on a plane to Sacramento." He shrugged his shoulders. "Sorry but I sorta eavesdropped on her phone call."

"I'm obliged for your kindness." Rod said shaking the man's hand.

Then he stood to leave and everyone in the Tavern/Restaurant waited at the door to shake his hand as he and Sonni walked outside.

He tightened Junior's cinch. Then he turned to face her.

"Thank you, Mister Rod Gantry," she said. You truly are a real Cowboy. And you saved my life, in more ways than one."

"Stay safe," he said.

He hopped into the stirrup, swung a leg over and pointed the appaloosa northeast out of Patagonia.

SET ME FREE

Courtney Gainer
Grand Island, FL

Life wasn't always like this. I could remember days when I couldn't be happier. We used to be a real family, my parents and me. We would go out every Friday. We would laugh and have fun together. There were no lies. There were no secrets. There were no arguments. There was no hate. My parents used to be in love. I used to love them. I used to feel good about myself. Now there was nothing inside of me. There was nothing inside of any of us.

Another argument. That was why I had left. My parents were yelling at each other about something they probably didn't remember the reason for. I was so tired of their screaming, my dad's icy voice, my mother's soft yet firm with rage. When our family changed, I don't know. Maybe when my dad had gotten his new high paying job. Maybe when he started going away on business trips every weekend. Maybe when my mom found out about the affair. All I know is that I wanted to escape. My dad's keys were the first thing my eyes fell upon. I grabbed the keys to the Volvo and drove away before they noticed that I had left the room. As I sat down in the driver's seat I noticed the half empty beer bottle my dad had left in the cup holder. Without thinking I took a long swig.

The drink was warm from staying in the car for so long. I didn't really care about the taste though. All I cared about was that after the first few sips I started to fall into a sort of weightlessness. A thick fog enveloped my mind. I couldn't see straight, couldn't even think straight. I didn't care. If I couldn't think straight, then I couldn't think of the argument, my grades falling, the darkness that had surrounded my family. I didn't even notice when I drove right off the side of the road. I did notice the pain that surged through me when I crashed into a tree. Bright lights appeared behind me, red and blue. I couldn't compile a coherent sentence. It didn't take much for the officer to realize that I was drunk.

When they put me in a cell I just sank down to the floor. They would call my parents. My father would be furious. I would be grounded for a long time. I would be lucky if he even came to get me out of jail. I didn't care. I didn't care about anything anymore.

"*Come with me,*" a voice whispered. It sounded vaguely like a snake hissing in my ear. I didn't think I heard it at first, none of the nearby officers seemed to, but then I heard it again. "*If you come with me, then you won't have to worry about anything anymore. Not your parents, not school, nothing. All you have to do is come with me and I'll take your suffering away. All you have to do is let the darkness in and I will make it all better."* I didn't know what to do, but the promise of ending my hurt was all I had wanted. I closed my eyes and just let the darkness overwhelm me.

The next thing I knew the sun was beating down on my skin with unrelenting heat. I opened my eyes and saw that I wasn't in the jail cell anymore. I felt instantly grateful for the change of scenery. That is, until I saw where I was. I was in a desert. All I could see was barren wasteland. The heat had burned away all life. Then I saw that I wasn't the only one there. There were several other people about ten feet apart. They all looked warn, like they had been in this wasteland for too long and the sun had turned them into raisin. I thought they were dead at first until I saw them move ever so slightly. They made a metal clanking noise when they moved. I realized that they all had manacles locked around their ankles and wrists attached to a metal spike in the burning ground. I looked down and saw that I had the same accessories. I was a prisoner. We all were.

"Where am I?" I called out to no one in particular. None of the people around me seemed to hear. If they did, then they ignored me. I tried again, "Please, someone tell me what happened!"

My only answer was a whispered laugh. I looked in every direction. My eyes fell onto a man to my right. His eyes grew wide with fear. I hadn't been the only one to hear the voice this time. "Who is he? Who was it that just laughed? The one that told me he could save me?"

The man's voice shook as he spoke. "He is the Dark One." I had to strain my ears to here him. "He is the ruler over this dominion and now all of our souls. There is no escape from this wretched place." The man sobbed, covering his face with his hands.

I saw something move out of the corner of my eyes. I turned to see a shadow moving across the desert. As it approached I noticed that it wasn't the only one. There were dozens of shadows that converged on each man and woman that lay on the rocky ground. When they surrounded me I saw that they were not just shadows but little demons. They had an impish figure and glowing red eyes. They collapsed on us hungrily. The pain was excruciating until the darkness pulled me in.

I couldn't see anything. Darkness surrounded me. I couldn't even see my own two hands. I was scared, more scared than I had ever been before. "Hello?" I asked the darkness. Something moved in the pitch black. I couldn't make out what it was. It seemed to be the darkness itself. All I knew was that I wasn't alone.

An eerie laugh danced all around me. It came from nowhere yet everywhere. It was the same voice as before. The voice of the Dark One. "How do you like my domain? Spacious, isn't it?" I turned to see who was speaking, but my eyes could make nothing out of the night.

My hands were shaking as I answered, "Where am I? What is this place?"

"This is where I live and where the people that have given me their souls now live. Including you."

"I never gave you my soul!" Hate surged through me, giving me strength and squelching the fear. Hate was better than fear, more powerful.

"Yes, you did. From the moment you took your father's keys, from the moment you drank the beer, from the moment you asked me to take it all away; you have been mine and always will be."

At that moment I woke up. I was back in the barren wasteland, the sun was shining and I could see the other people around me. The Dark One was nowhere to be seen. I looked out into the desert, thinking about the life I had lost because of my mistakes. I knew that I would never see my parents again. I would never see my friends. I would never get the chance to do better in school. My parents were likely to get a divorce when they found out about my mysterious disappearance. After that, who knew what would happen to them? I looked up into the sky and saw something flying in the vast horizon. It was a bird, a dove from what I could tell. I wished I could fly away from this place. "Please," I whispered, "please set me free."

I didn't know how much time passed. The sun didn't move in the sky above us. It always stayed a constant afternoon, the hottest part of the day. Night never came to cool down the desert. The only way I could tell that another day had passed was when the shadows descended on us again, dragging us back into the darkness that didn't bring comfort to the ever-present heat.

He was there again when the night came. His voice sounded on edge. "Is this not what you wanted? All I did was what you asked."

"I never asked for this!"

"Of course it is. You asked me to take away all of your problems, all of your suffering. I have done that. You no longer have to think about your parents or your grades. There is no reason for them in this place. I told you all you had to do was let the darkness in, and you did. That was not my doing, it was your choice."

"This isn't what I wanted. Set me free!" I raced through the darkness, desperately searching for a way out, for some sort of light. My feet were moving, but it seemed as though my feet were not taking me so far as an inch.

"No one can save you now!"

I was suddenly back in the desert. All of my hope seemed to have drained out of my veins and replaced with a cold numbness of surrender. There was nothing I could do. The shackles had no key hole. I could not slip my wrists away. The Dark One would not release me no matter how much I begged. I was a prisoner of the darkness for the rest of eternity. I placed my face in my hands and cried.

Then I heard a cooing sound. I slowly lifted my head to see a bird perched on the spike that was attached to my chains. It was the same dove as before. I lifted my hand slowly and stroked its pure white feathers. "How

I wish you could give me your wings. I would give anything to escape this place, to be back with my family." Then the bird suddenly flew away off into the distance. My heart ached to join the dove.

A bright light appeared in the same direction the bird had flown. I squinted but could not make out what it was coming from. As the light came closer, brighter, I heard a loud noise. The demons that took us into the darkness every night were cowering, shrieking in fear and anger. Then I heard the Dark One's cry join them. Whatever was coming did not make him happy

When the light was a few feet away I could finally make out the figure draped in white light. It was a man. He looked worn with the age of the centuries but as young as someone not forty years old. In my heart I know who he was. I knew that this man, the one the dark creatures feared, could save me. "Set me free! Jesus, rescue me!"

At my cry he turned towards me. Jesus stared into my eyes and I was captured by his gaze. He looked straight into my mind, through lies, my anger, all of the darkness that had clouded my life. He stood before me and held out his hand. "Do you want to be free? Live in me and I will rid you of your sins. Let the light of my love extinguish the darkness of the Dark One." Slowly, I placed my hand in his. As I did the chains on my ankles and wrists disintegrated into a fine dust. I rose to my feet and stood before my Savior. He turned to the rest of the ones around us. "Do you want to be free?" he rose his voice for all to hear. "Lift your chains and let my light relieve you of your burdens!" The man that had spoken to me the other day got up and lifted his shackles. Several others followed him, but, Jesus was sad to see, not all rose. Then, Jesus turned to me. "Let's go home."

I opened my eyes to see that I was back in the cell at the jail. I looked at my watch and saw that not a minute had passed since I had heard the voice. I looked around me, confused. "Did all of that just really happen?" I whispered to myself. Then I realized my heart, it felt lighter somehow. I knew that I was saved.

A police officer came to open my cell and motioned me to follow him. Waiting for me was my mother and father. Instead of the anger that I had expected I saw worry.

"Are you alright? What happened? We were worried sick about you!" My parents were talking at the same time, not giving me enough time to form a sentence. I heard a love in their voice that I hadn't heard in a long time. I ran over to them and hugged them. "Are you alright?" my mother asked again. I nodded into her shoulder feeling tears well up in my eyes.

"I'm just glad to be home."

THE NOMADS

Yvette Ward-Horner
Cody, WY

Dawn had pearled the sky but the woods still lay in shadow when they turned on to the track leading up to the house. The pick-up bounced and squeaked on the rough red road.

The child leaned against the dusty window, her temple knocking the glass with every rut. Her yellow hair was rumpled and damp with sweat. The truck dipped suddenly in a pothole and her head cracked hard against the window frame. Little needles of pain shot through her forehead. She looked viciously at her mother, who was leaning over the wheel, her dress bunched up and wrinkled around her thighs. Her neck drooped and her head bounced up and down.

The child turned away, sneering, and slouched down in her seat, watching the road through half-closed, glittering eyes. Her resentment burned a steady hole in her gut.

When the truck slowed down she sat up a little, furtively trying to get a better look. A faded white ranch house slumped at the edge of a clearing, its paint peeling and gutters hanging askew. Weeds had claimed a small stack of tires by the porch. The child viewed the scene through the curtain of her lashes, intent on concealing her interest. Her mouth tasted bitter and she gnawed at her lip. Having seen it all, she shut her eyes and feigned sleep.

Her mother turned the truck around in the dirt in front of the house before parking off to one side by the patchy grass. She reached across and tapped her daughter on the shoulder. The child snorted and blew a little bubble for effect, then heaved up and scowled at her mother. A dark crust had built up in the corners of her faded blue eyes and her round face was swollen and flushed.

"We're here," her mother said in a high voice.

The child glanced indifferently at the scene outside the window, then opened her door abruptly and plunged out. Her sandals sank into the long wet grass and she felt the dew soak quickly through her socks. Face set, she stomped across the dirt to the front of the house and stood waiting bunched up on the porch. Her mother got out too and lingered close to the truck, looking all around with an air of wonder. The child hunched her shoulders and glared at her feet, feeling hot and explosive with contempt. On an impulse, she pushed the doorbell hard.

The man who flung the door wrathfully open wore sweatpants hung low on his hips. He stared at the child as if he'd never seen anything like her. She stared back, sucking on the inside of her cheek.

Then they heard her mother's cry split through the morning air and the man's head jerked up as if on a spring.

"Janice!" he exclaimed and his color drained.

"Jack," she said, beginning to weep. "We only came 'cause we're broke – we got no place to go." Her mouth trembled and she held out her arms with a whimper.

The child rolled her eyes as the man sprang down the steps, his odor of bed sweat blowing over her. She watched him grab her mother and kiss her hard.

"Stupid, stupid, dumb," she muttered blackly.

She turned away to the open door and peered into the hallway, her attention caught by a movement in the gloom. A woman appeared, rubbing her eyes, and drifted like a ghost onto the porch. She glanced at the child with absent resignation. The child followed her gaze out to the pick-up, where her mother stood close to the man, their heads bent together, deep in conversation. They didn't notice the woman as she approached them. The child crept after her with eager cunning, holding her hands together in front of her chest. Her lips trembled with anticipation.

Suddenly her mother looked up and jumped when she saw the woman; the man looked over his shoulder and gaped. *Now*, thought the child, *she's going to get it*.

But the woman simply smiled at the man inquiringly.

"Morning, Bess," he said, flushing. "Looks like we've got us a couple of guests."

The woman nodded slowly and said nothing.

"Bess, this is Janice," the man said loudly. "A real old friend of mine. And this here is Elspeth, her girl. I'd like y'all to meet Bessie, my wife."

"Pleased to meetcha," Bess said, looking from one to the other. "I expect y'all are pretty hungry for breakfast." She adjusted her house robe with plump brown hands, pulling the faded blue terrycloth over her breasts. Then she motioned for them to follow her into the kitchen.

A wide green field edged with woods lay behind the house and after breakfast the child went out to play in it. She lay on her back in the tall, coarse grass and frowned up at the shimmering sky. Her mother was in love again, this time with Jack. Nothing ever went right when her mother was in love.

She wondered if she could run away and get a pick-up of her own to drive around in. She liked trucks, they had always been part of her life. She still missed their last truck; it had been all one color with a soft cracked leather seat. Before that had been the powder blue one, leaking spots of grease wherever they parked it. There had been a man then who drove around with them; smelling of engine oil and Old Spice cologne. His face had been scratchy when she kissed him goodnight and he had called her The Little Potato. The child remembered his face but not his name.

A sudden noise approaching interrupted her thoughts – the sound of someone swishing through the grass. The child shut her eyes and held herself still. The swishing grew closer, then circled around her, and finally came to a stop right by her head.

"Are you dead?" a young voice asked with interest.

The child's eyes flew open and she made a hideous face, scrunching up her lips and baring her teeth. The boy standing over her stared in amazement. The child kept it up for as long as she could, then collapsed feeling faintly embarrassed.

"Well, I guess you're not dead," the boy said calmly.

"No, but my dad is!" snapped the child.

The boy sat down in the grass and looked at her and the child stared reluctantly back. He had warm brown hair and a mole above his eyebrow, his eyes were the color of the sky. He looked as clean and wholesome as pasteurized milk.

"What did he die of?" he said.

The child shrugged, narrowing her eyes, and wished he would mind his own business.

"You do too know," he said and watched her.

"He got hit by a train," the child said, scowling. "He was dizzy and he walked out on the tracks."

"He was drunk, you mean." The boy crinkled up his eyes. "My dad gets drunk on Fridays."

"Who cares about your dad?" the child said, turning away. "I never asked you nothing about him."

"You'd better care about him, 'cause you're staying in his house." The boy gazed at her watchfully. "You and your mother both," he added. "So you'd better care or else he'll throw you out."

The child absorbed this and lay back down, feeling that she had reached an impasse.

"Aren't you going to say something?" the boy asked after a while and the child shook her head in gloomy silence. "Do you care about my dad now?" he asked her.

"No!" she said. "And I never will neither. Nobody cares about *me*."

"That's 'cause you're like a porcupine," the boy said. "Or a pricker bush, or . . . " He ran out of inspiration. "I'm going to look for owls," he said. "You can come if you want. My dad said I had to be nice to you."

The child shook her head and rolled over, turning her back to the boy. She waited for him to persuade her. But instead he just said "See you later," and left.

That night, lying alone in the hard bed she shared with her mother, the child wept silent angry tears. She had waited all day for the boy to come back and talk to her but she hadn't seen him again until suppertime. He had smiled at her across the table and asked her to pass the salt and she had done so with a flat accusing scowl. Bess had frowned and asked her to try to be pleasant.

Thinking of Bess, the child shivered a little. There would be trouble there in the days that were yet to come. It was her practice to see everything without seeming to notice a thing and that night she had seen how Bess looked at her mother. Grim suspicion had drained the warmth from the woman's small brown eyes, now grown hard and flat and wary like a snake's. Bess had watched Jack and the child's mother all night, never once joining in their conversation. The child had seen the woman's anger seething behind her face and it made her hands cold. She'd watched along with Bess as her mother giggled selfishly with Jack and she'd longed to grab her hair and drag her out of there. As soon as dinner was over, she had slunk up to their room and it seemed safe in there – dark and somehow familiar.

She was still awake hours later when her mother finally crept in and through half-closed eyes she watched her change for bed. Her mother spent a long time brushing her hair, humming little snatches of a love song. The child waited until her mother was climbing in beside her and then snorted and heaved like a walrus under the blanket. Her mother jumped and clutched her chest, then sat very still for a minute. The child lay quiet and eventually her mother sighed and muttered to herself; "Why me?"

Yes, why you, her daughter thought, clenching her fists. *Nobody hates you as much as I do.*

The next day dragged by, long and slow and hot, and then another just like it and another. Apparently her mother had set up shop. The child found a spot in the field and went to it every day, whiling away the hours braiding grass. Day after day she watched Jack and her mother walk through the field to the woods and sometimes she noticed Bess looking out of the window.

One day the boy came out and apologized for neglecting her, obviously sent by his watchful mother. The child said *Never mind* and he sat down by her legs, tearing up grass and twisting it in his fingers. The child saw he had something on his mind. Finally it came out – he had heard his mother crying in the bathroom.

"She never cries," he told the child, his eyes narrow and cloudy. "She didn't even cry when she broke her arm."

"My ma cries all the time," the child said. "Sometimes she cries when she's driving."

The boy shuddered. "Now why does she do that?" he asked her.

The child shrugged and gazed up at the sky. "She cries about my daddy all the time."

"'Cause he got hit by a train?"

"Nah," the child said. "It weren't a train – he got shot. I guess I was just lying about the train."

"How come he got shot?" gasped the boy, flushing. "Who shot him, then, another man?"

"Yeah, a man who came to our house at night."

The child paused, remembering. Gunfire boomed suddenly in her head.

"Shot him in the chest with a hunting rifle. " she said. "My ma saved his shirt. It still has blood on it. It was red at first but now it's kind of brown." She stared across the field, turning slightly pale. "I was little but I remember the whole thing," she added. She looked at him with a grimace.

The boy sat silent, slowly digesting her tale. He stared at her with newfound admiration.

"I'm almost twelve," he said at last. "And I've seen a lot of things in my life."

"Ain't never seen your daddy get shot," the child said and he couldn't reply to that.

From that time on the boy hovered constantly at her side and the child soon came to rely on his presence. She showed him where Jack and her mother snuck into the woods and he said he thought they must be looking for birds' nests. The child thought he must be naïve; she knew that they were probably having sex. Why else would two grown-ups sneak off into the trees, holding hands? The child had seen her mother having sex before – with big loud men who had hairy backs. She didn't know what exactly was involved in the process, but she knew that you had to be naked. She thought she'd be embarrassed to be naked.

The boy offered her a penny for her thoughts and after a moment she told him. She told him everything she knew or imagined about sex. His face glistened with sweat when she finished. The child considered telling him what his father did in the woods but could tell that it would get him in an uproar. He had a funny look on his face; his eyes half-closed and his mouth hanging loosely open. The child thought he looked like an overheated dog and she grinned with a strange feeling of power.

Copying something she had seen her mother do, she lay back in the grass and stretched her arms behind her head. The boy crawled over and kneeled beside her. He put a hand on her hair. The child smiled and suddenly he flopped down on top of her, his hands reaching blindly behind her head. The child gasped and tried to push him away. He was heavy like a big dog, pinning her down.

"Hey," she said. "Hey, what are you doing? Stop it, you're hurting my ribs!"

He stopped moving and lay silently on top of her, breathing into her hair.

"Don't you want to do it?" he said.

Do what? For a moment she blinked in bewilderment. Then she realized that he wanted to have sex. She thought quickly, surprised and flattered, then smiled a little smile he couldn't see.

"Not just yet," she said.

The next day, in the field, she let him kiss her hand, then her cheek and then, quickly, her mouth. He was panting in her ear by the time she kissed him back and his hot breath sent shivers down her spine.

"Come on," he pleaded. "Let's do it now. Don't you want to know what it feels like?"

She did, but she wouldn't admit it for the world and besides that it was too much fun controlling him. She kept on saying; "Not yet."

Three days later the child spied her mother walking slowly into the woods all by herself. Her shoulders drooped and the child thought gladly that Jack had probably dumped her. She got to her feet and crept along behind her. Her mother went to a clearing and sat on a fallen tree and the child hid behind a tangle of rhododendron. With disappointment she saw Jack making his way towards them. He walked up to her mother and embraced her. The child watched them kissing, pressed against each other – the sight made her trembly and ill. She saw Jack's hand sliding down her mother's back and it made her think of a nasty hairy spider.

Suddenly she jumped up and fled, crashing noisily through the undergrowth. She heard Jack shout hoarsely behind her, and her mother's wail of terror and dismay. Grinning fiercely, panting through her teeth, the child raced into the field and threw herself down. A few moments later Jack rushed past her; he didn't see her lying there and watching him. The child hugged herself and rolled over on her face, spraying her mirth into the dirt. She lay there laughing quietly to herself until she felt a sudden touch on the back of her leg.

Craning her head back, she saw the boy standing over her, his mouth hanging open in a now familiar way. He knelt beside her, smiling hopefully, and touched the back of her neck with a tentative hand.

The child's expression changed suddenly and grew almost violent in its intensity. She rolled onto her back and stared at him coldly. Then she threw one of her legs a little to the side. The boy froze instantly, a stunned look on his face, and his breath began to come faster.

"You have to be naked," the child said.

He nodded slowly and unzipped his pants, shedding them without embarrassment. The child darted a quick look at his clean white underpants, then closed her eyes and turned her head away. She heard his shirt rustle as he discarded it on the grass and then he started tugging at her buttons.

"I don't have to be naked till I'm older!" she said angrily and pushed him away. She began to fumble with her jeans.

At that moment the sky seemed to suddenly shatter inwards, as a great leaping shadow covered the sun. The child felt herself picked up and thrown down again; she fell into the grass screaming helplessly. Someone else was screaming too and she heard the loud smack of hand against flesh. Hysterical, the child saw the boy running naked toward the house and then Bess, his angry mother, towered over her. The child cowered and tried to twist away as Bess seized her by the arm and yanked her up.

"You're a dirty little tramp, just like your ma," Bess said in fury. "The two of you are getting out of my house."

The child choked and enormous tears ran hotly down her face, her chest heaved and hiccupped uncontrollably.

"Look at you," Bess said. Her mouth twisted. "You're nothing but a bawling little baby. And here you are in my own yard, diddling with my boy."

The child opened her mouth and howled, her face turning purple. Bess pushed her roughly toward the house.

"Get your things and put them in the truck," she said. "I want you out of here right now."

The pick-up rolled past the endless tobacco fields, a small speck of red in all the green. The child sat staring out of the window, her fingers knitted loosely in her lap. Her mother was tight-lipped, hunched stiffly over the wheel; she kept her angry eyes fixed on the road.

"I could of married him," she said, clenching her jaw. "I could of married him and lived in that house."

The child frowned at the road. She was sick of hearing it.

"I could of married him but for you," her mother said loudly.

Rage boiled up suddenly inside the child. She clenched her fists but couldn't keep it down. Red-faced, she flung around and glared at her mother.

"He weren't yours to marry!" she shrieked at the top of her voice. "He weren't yours to marry in the first place!"

Her mother gasped as though she'd been slapped and her eyes brimmed over with instant tears.

"Don't you speak to me like that," she whispered furiously.

"He weren't yours to marry," the child repeated. "You had no right."

"What do you know about it?" cried her mother. "I knew him before she ever came along. I knew him first and I loved him and he loved me!"

The child subsided and turned back to the window, gritting her teeth.

"I could of married him," her mother said again and began to weep with abandon.

The child reached over and snapped on the radio, drowning out the sound of her mother's tears.

WHEN GANGSTERS BURN YOUR HOUSE DOWN WITH YOU IN IT
(MANUSCRIPT EXCERPT)

Karen Duffy
Ventnor, NJ

Imagine this.

It's 6:30 on Saturday morning and your house is on fire. But it's no longer "a fire on the front porch." It's "the house is on fire," and that's different. Joe has said everyone has to get out and you can rely on Joe's sense of danger because he's a combat veteran. He speaks in words like "incoming" and "hot LZ" and "Charlie Alpha." If Joe says it's time to get out, it's time to get out.

It's now only about two minutes since Megan ran into our room to say there was a fire outside on the front porch. How does a fire start on the front porch? And how did Megan know there was a fire? Later we'll learn that she'd fallen asleep on the living room sofa and had heard the flames. She heard the crackling because the sofa was on the other side of the wall from where the fire was. She'd only slept there by accident.

It's 6:30 in the morning and I'm back in our bedroom. If I'm back in our bedroom, I must've passed all the kids' rooms to get there because our bedroom's at the far end of the hall from the stairs. But I don't remember going there. This part, though, this I remember.

I stood in our bedroom with my Uggs on, and I had to wake up the kids. I moved down the hall to Mike's bedroom. I woke Mike up first. Mike, my 15-year-old son, was in the bedroom closest to the steps, the escape route, but farthest away from where I stood in my bedroom, and I got him first. What I'm saying is that I deliberately passed the bedrooms of my two other children even though they were on the way, in order to get Mike first. This was not something I was conscious of at the time, but something I thought about later after I realized I had done it. Why had I done that? What did it mean? That I loved him the most?

Anyone with more than one child knows that children take turns as the focus of a parent's worries. When one of your kids is having a good year in school, the other doesn't have enough friends. And when the other suddenly has friends, the first one doesn't make the team. At 6:30 on that Saturday morning, I was most worried about Mike. I tell myself today that this is the reason I passed by the other two to get him first.

Mike was shy, self-conscious, and spacey. He'd always had a helpless-in-the-world quality that made me just want to explode with love. Every time his sister called him a "dork," I was afraid she was right.

Mike hadn't adjusted as well as I'd hoped when we moved to Ventnor four years earlier. That was when Joe and I had first moved in together. Even though Mike's father and I had been separated for over three years, the move to Ventnor came not long after the divorce was final. Plus--and I should've known this--I'd underestimated how much tougher Ventnor was than the inland community we'd come from. Out there, Mike played the trumpet, and was on the soccer team. He had Umbros in several colors. But in Ventnor, the only thing less cool than soccer clothes was playing the trumpet. Surfing clothes and surfing were cool, not playing in the band, and other sixth-graders let him know it. Now he was in tenth grade and even though he'd had athletic, and therefore, social success, I still worried about him.

I leaned into his door with my shoulder because it always stuck. The house was old and crooked.

"Mike--get up. The house is on fire."

"Huh?"

"The house is on fire! We have to get out!"

"What do you mean?"

"Mike! The house is on fire and we have to get out!"

"It's on fire? Why?

"Mike! Get up!"

I saw him begin to sit up and swing his legs over the side of the bed, so I ran down to Lexie's room, *still* passing by two-year-old Bryan's room. I must've known Joe would get Bryan, which he did, that same minute, though I don't remember him doing it.

Lexie's name is really Alexandra, which means Warrior Woman. She was thirteen and in seventh grade, confident, loud, and fast on her feet. I knew that even if I woke her up last, she'd be out first. And she was. A minute later, Mike was running down the steps and I was behind him. But I couldn't find Lex. I would search many more times that morning for people I'd already found, repeating a frantic cycle of search, find, forget; search, find, forget. I must have replayed the steps in this endless loop forty times between 6:30 and about 9:00AM. Finally I spotted Lex, already outside, halfway down the street with Bryan in her arms.

But this fire, this house. It was always too good to be true. All of the renovations. How did Toglia afford them? Why did he sell the house to us? There were stories about him, but...it's Atlantic City. Everybody tells stories. But now—the County Prosecutor's been looking for something we might have. Yesterday—no, the day before—there was another article in the paper, but we were scared to call. We had to talk about it first. What if we were guilty, too? We worked for the same school district as Toglia, but we were teachers. He was a groundskeeper. We never saw him at work. We hardly knew him at all.

I stood in the kitchen near the back door, the door everyone had escaped from. I knew Joe was still in the house because I remember hearing his voice telling me to get out. Did he still have Bryan? I don't know. I think Joe had given him to Lex or to Megan at that point. But I remember standing there in our kitchen, my kitchen, and looking out across the living room toward the front porch --and seeing smoke come through the walls. All of the smoke detectors in the house went off at the same time. Had Megan not slept on the sofa, this would have been our first warning.

In accidental fires, smoke comes at the *beginning* of the fire. There is a period of smoldering and smoking which smoke detectors detect. But because our fire started outside and traveled straight up, the entire outside of the house on both floors was engulfed before *any* smoke came into the house and set off alarms. In our case, a mass of flames and noxious smoke announced itself all at once.

Had Megan not slept on the sofa, we wouldn't have known the fire was out there. We would've been asleep, just as we'd been three-four minutes earlier. We would've had about one minute to get out. From asleep to outside in less than a minute, six of us. Possible, yes. I think it was possible. The firemen would later say probably not.

Bryan's bedroom , in the middle, was the smallest bedroom. It was situated across the front of the house to allow for the space that made the upstairs hallway. The effect inside his room was not just that it was smaller, but that it was pushed forward, closer to the windows. Proportionately, the windows were big. In the summer, it was the coolest room in the house because it seemed to be all window. All front window. Bryan's crib, and, therefore, Bryan himself, was less than five feet from those windows.

Later my husband would tell me that when he went in to get Bryan out of his crib, which was the same moment I was waking up Lex, Bryan was already half awake. When Bryan saw Joe's face, he broke into his moonfaced grin and stuck his arms out to play the bouncy game they played every morning. But Joe leaned over and said, "Not today, Buddy." All he could see out Bryan's windows was orange. It was a wall of fire. I remember expressing surprise later that the fire could've grown that quickly. I couldn't believe flames had been "licking" at Bryan's windows in what seemed like a matter of seconds. Joe, who is not one to exaggerate, said, "They weren't licking. It was a huge, orange wall."

That was less than four minutes after Megan had come into our room.

I stood in the kitchen in a spot where I could see the front door and the back door at the same time and heard the smoke detectors go off. I heard Joe tell me to get out. I heard windows break. I saw thick, black smoke oozing through the living room walls. I am not talking about airy, atmospheric, campfire smoke that hangs in the air like fog. I am talking about a solid mass of pitch-black poison. Oily, thick, toxic, refinery smoke, the kind you can't take one breath of. Not one. That's what was oozing through the front walls of my house like terrifying, vengeful anger, and behind it, violent, living, breathing flames.

And this is what I've been wanting to say. This is what you have to think about.

It is 6:30 in the morning. It is Saturday. You are in your kitchen. This is the place where you live, the place that feeds you and holds you, and this place-- is going to kill you. This fire, this smoke, is coming into your house and you have to let it. You have to let it come in, and you have to get out.

THE MILL STREET GANG

Norma Laughter
Rutherfordton, NC

The raucous crowd gathers,
having harassed a hapless hawk
into seeking safer hunting
several 'hoods away.
Boisterous, brazen, bullies all,
and quite celebratory
after a good mobbing!
Masters of trash talk,
these hecklers have declared
open season on peace and quiet.
Strutting smart and shotgun savvy,
crows were gangstas
before gangstas were cool.

CONSTELLATION

Marla Alupoaicei
Frisco, TX

> *Two forces prevail in the universe: light and gravity.*
> —Simone Weil

A moth pinned to halogen. Oracle.
Dusty wings, martyred light.
A body's need for oxygen, each breath a minor miracle.
Lucent navigation, our cartography of flight.

Pure luminosity torches the dark.
Starcraft of motion, insomnia's rhyme.
The glittering geode of my heart,
sailing bright oceans on borrowed time.

Pendulum of cave-pearl moon,
pungency of burning moth.
Tides subsiding all too soon,
loosened pleats of space-time's cloth.

All I thought was near is far.
We'll never know the final cost.
Sparks rebound from all you are—
the patron saint of all things lost.

What it feels like to go home:
a domain that we can call *ours*.
Cassiopeia's chained to her throne:
a paradox of stars.

RACE RELATIONS

By Carrie Printz
Denver, CO

ACT I
SCENE 1

(The Porter Herald-News office. Old rock 'n
roll and movie posters line the walls. One of
them, ideally, is "All the President's Men." A bar
or two of '80s music plays in the background.

Jen Hayes sits at a desk, typing rapidly on a
typewriter. She is driven, intense and wired
from caffeine. She munches fast-food as she
types. Max Cohen, cocky and equally intense,
is doing a headstand against the back wall.

Enter Will Martinez, laid-back compared to
these two. He wanders in and stares at Max for
a moment, then approaches Jen. She continues
typing and does not look up as he starts to talk.)

WILL

Excuse me?

JEN

Yep.

WILL

Are you one of the editors?

JEN

Yep.

WILL

Hi. I'm Will.

                    (He extends his hand, but Jen ignores
                    it and continues to type.)

JEN

Hi.

WILL

Is this a bad time? I can come back.

JEN

It's always a bad time. What's on your mind?

WILL

I'd like to write for the paper.

JEN

Got any experience?

WILL

No, but I've been told I'm a good writer and...

JEN

Don't tell me. You're a freshman.

WILL

Uh-huh.

JEN

You look a little old to be a freshman.

WILL

I am. I'm 22. I served.

JEN

Served what?

                         WILL
You know--in the military.

                         JEN
Oh.

                         WILL
Plus, I had a year of junior college.

                      (A Pause.)

                   WILL (Continued)
I know. You're wondering what a guy like me is doing at a place like Porter.

                         JEN
Not really.

                         WILL
It's okay. Sometimes I do too. What can I say? I got lucky. Plus I worked my
butt off

                         JEN
Good for you...Look, most of us here worked on our high school paper...In
fact, most of us were the editors.

                         WILL
Oh.

                         JEN
That's not to say there isn't a place for you.

                         WILL
Great!

                         JEN
You just have to start at the bottom. News briefs and stuff like that.

                      (Max, still in a headstand, suddenly starts
                      humming loudly. Will turns to look at him.)

WILL
(to Jen)

Is he okay?

JEN

Max? He's fine. He's just getting ready to write his column. It psychs him up.

WILL

Max? Max Cohen? I'm a big fan.

(Max drops out of his headstand
and pats Will on the back.)

MAX

Jen, give this man a job.

WILL

I read your column every week.

MAX
(to Jen)

Bright guy.

WILL

Of course, I usually disagree with you.

MAX

Oh...

WILL

But you're refreshing. The lone conservative voice at Porter. (to Jen) No offense, but everything else in the paper reads like it was written by the same person.

MAX

So true.

JEN

You think you can do better…What did you say your name was again?

WILL

Will. I don't know. Maybe. I'd like to try.

MAX

I like this guy. Give him a chance. We were green once too.

JEN

Speak for yourself.

MAX

I forgot. You did your first interview at 2. Sitting in Daddy's lap, right?

JEN
Shut up.

MAX
(to Will)

Daddy's a well-known journalist.

WILL

Cool. Who?

JEN

It's not important. What if I gave you a try-out? Do you have any ideas?

WILL

I don't know…maybe an interview with President Hall?

JEN

Forget it. We've been trying to talk to her for the past month. She's too busy.

WILL

I think she'll talk to me.

JEN

What makes you so special?

WILL

I know her pretty well.

MAX

How does a lowly freshman know the president of the university?

WILL

I met her my first day on campus. Just walked up and introduced myself.

JEN

She remembers you? I've met her like four or five
times and she never remembers me.

MAX

Maybe you just don't make that much of an impression, Jen.

(Jen shoots Max an angry glance.)

WILL

She's really nice. She invited me to dinner at her house. John Updike was
there. It was great.

MAX

Updike? Ah, man…What was he like?

WILL

Interesting. We talked music. He's really into punk. Patti Smith. The Clash.

MAX

No way!

WILL

Sure—he likes to hang out in the mosh pit at concerts.

JEN

Yeah, right.

WILL

Okay, I'm kidding. But we did talk about music--and art and books. Smart
guy.

JEN

I can't believe you had dinner at her house!

                              MAX

You'll have to excuse Jennifer. She worships President Hall.

                              JEN

She's an amazing woman…

                    (Max, knowing the rest of this speech
                    joins in, imitating Jen's enthusiasm.)

                         JEN and MAX

Grew up poor. Graduated magna cum laude from Yale. First black woman
president of a major university.

                             WILL

She's impressive, all right.

                              JEN

I just figured it out!

                             WILL

What?

                              JEN

Why she invited you to dinner…You're poor! You're here on scholarship.

                              MAX

Careful, Jen.

                             WILL

She's right. But I'd like to think it was my charming personality that got me
invited the first time.

                              JEN

You've been more than once?

                             WILL

Just twice.

                              MAX

Unbelievable.

                              49

                              WILL
I think I'm sort of a poster child.

                              JEN
For what?

                              WILL
You know—poor kid from East L.A. Works hard. Gets into elite university.

                              JEN
                            (excited)
I can see it now…You'll interview President Hall about her early life in
Mississippi. Then weave in stuff about your own struggles. You did have
struggles, right?

                              WILL
Sure. But I don't know if I want to write about them.

                              JEN
Trust me. People love that stuff.

                              MAX
All the bleeding hearts around here will eat it up.

                              JEN
Just ignore him. That's what I do.

                              MAX
                            (to Will)
She's secretly in love with me.

                              JEN
                            (to Will)
You'd never know Max was a socialist freshman year. Even had a poster of Karl
Marx above his bed.

                              MAX
                      (to Will, conspiratorially)
Don't ask how she knows this.

                            JEN
I'll edit your story. I'll make it sing! What do you say?

                              (Will starts to answer but is interrupted by
                              Shauna Johnson, who marches angrily into
                              the office with a newspaper in her hands. She
                              slams it down on a desk in front of Max.)

                          SHAUNA
What the hell is this crap, Cohen?

                            MAX
Looks like my column, Johnson.

                          SHAUNA
Accusing us of racism? Where do you get off?

                            MAX
It's called freedom of the press. Maybe you've heard of it?

                          SHAUNA
You mean freedom to lie.

                            MAX
I stand by everything I wrote.

                          SHAUNA
                         (indignant)
The African-American Student Association is not a racist organization.

                            MAX
Did I say that?

                          SHAUNA
It's implied.

                            MAX
I call 'em as I see 'em.

SHAUNA

You're a racist little twerp.

JEN

Shauna, let's not get personal.

SHAUNA
(to Jen)

What are you going to do about this? His columns are getting more and more
inflammatory. People are really pissed off.

MAX

You don't like it—write a letter to the editor.

SHAUNA

We never denied you entry to our meeting. That's a complete lie!

MAX

I was told I was not welcome. What's the difference? I had every right to
be there, and I was asked not to come in because I'm not black. If that's not
reverse racism, I don't know what is.

SHAUNA

You weren't welcome because you're an asshole, Cohen.

MAX

Is that in your bylaws? No assholes allowed?

(Will starts to laugh.)

SHAUNA
(to Will)

Who the hell are you?

WILL

Um, nobody.

SHAUNA

Do you think this is funny?

WILL

No. It's just a nervous reflex. When people fight, I start to laugh.

SHAUNA

That's too bad. Because there's nothing funny about this. (to Max) You're a dangerous person, Cohen, because you're ignorant. And we don't want you anywhere near our meetings.

MAX

If I'm so ignorant, maybe you should have let me in. You could have educated me.

SHAUNA

You just would have twisted something people said and used it for your own agenda.

MAX

And what's that?

SHAUNA

Self-promotion. Mixed with hatred. (to Jen) I'd like a full retraction, but I know I'm not going to get one. Ideally, I'd like him kicked off the paper.

JEN

You know that's not going to happen. If you don't like his opinion, don't read it.

SHAUNA

You're going to keep running this stuff?

(Jen nods.)

SHAUNA (Continued, to Jen)

We're going to have a problem.

JEN

I guess so.

SHAUNA

You people do not want to take me on.

                              MAX

I'm trembling.

                            SHAUNA

I'm serious. My Dad's a libel lawyer in D.C. He's gone after the big boys. CBS.
The Washington Post. You guys are small potatoes.

                              MAX

I stand by everything I wrote.

                            SHAUNA

Who cares? My Dad comes after you, you'll wish you'd never set foot in this
office.

                              MAX

Sounds like a great guy. Can't wait to meet him.

                            SHAUNA

You know what I can't stand more than an ignorant racist?

                              MAX

What?

                            SHAUNA

A glib, pompous windbag.

                              MAX
                            (laughs)
That's the best you can do? Can't you be a little more inventive? I thought you
were an English major.

                            SHAUNA

Poli Sci. Give me time. I'll think of something better.

                              MAX

I look forward to it.

                            SHAUNA

You people…

(Shauna turns and exits indignantly.)

WILL

Man, she's a little scary.

MAX

I like her. Plus. I think she wants me. Did you see how she kept avoiding looking me in the eye? A tell-tale sign.

JEN

Is there no end to your ego? Maybe you ought to tone it down for a while. Go back to something less controversial.

WILL

Yeah, I loved your column about bowling not being a real sport. I bet you didn't offend too many people with that one.

MAX

You'd be surprised…Guys, I'm not backing down now. Things are just heating up! We're talking protests, sit-ins, TV coverage…just what this campus needs! I say, bring it on!

(Jen and Will look at each other.)

END SCENE

SCENE 2

(Herald-News office. A week later. Jen is on the phone, listening to an earful from the other end. Will enters. Jen slams down the phone.)

JEN

You can drop dead too! You loser!

(Jen slams the phone on the receiver several more times for effect.)

WILL

Uh, hi. You okay?

JEN

Max's latest column. We're getting a lot of calls.

WILL

I saw the graffiti on the wall outside too. "Die Hate Mongers!" Nice.

JEN

He's completely lost his mind. He's got a death wish or something.

WILL

Yeah—taking on black sororities and fraternities. That's pretty bold. Although...you guys did choose to run his column.

JEN

Right. So, if anything happens to him, it's my fault.

WILL

You don't think anyone would actually hurt him? Over a newspaper column?

JEN

We've had threats.

WILL

Just some angry kids blowing off steam.

JEN

I hope you're right.

(Will picks up the day's paper and opens to Max's column.)

WILL

I can't believe he quotes Martin Luther King. Then accuses the university of segregation for supporting black sororities and fraternities? The guy's got nerve—I'll give him that...I love this part...(He reads from the paper.) "I invite my black brothers and sisters to break the color barrier, leave their all-black tables in the cafeteria and join me some time on the all-white side. Is this Mississippi 1962 or Porter University 1985?"

(Will sets down the paper.)

WILL (Continued)

He doesn't exactly shy away from controversy, does he?

JEN

Are you kidding? He seeks it out like a missile...I'm getting this massive migraine. I think I'm gonna hear from Shauna Johnson before the day's over.

WILL

There is some truth to what he's saying...About the tables in the cafeteria.

JEN

Maybe.

WILL

I don't know you that well. But just a guess here--When's the last time you had dinner with your best black girlfriend?

(Jen doesn't answer.)

WILL (Continued)

Uh-huh.

JEN

Where do you fit into all this? Where do you sit at meals?

WILL

There aren't really enough of us here to have a strong presence--yet. You don't see any Hispanic fraternities or sororities. I just hang out with everyone.

JEN

That doesn't sound so bad.

WILL

It's not. I like you people, in general. But there's always a part of you that wonders if you're really welcome at the party. Plus, you guys cannot make a decent burrito to save your life.

JEN

A lot of us have plenty of guilt. For everything we've done—and are still doing.

WILL

My heart breaks for you. It's tough being a privileged, liberal white American. You have everything you could possibly want, but you still feel guilty about it.

JEN

Can we change the subject? My headache is getting worse.

WILL

Here's some good news. I got the interview with President Hall. Day after tomorrow.

JEN

That's great!

WILL

Plus, she invited me to dinner again. Tomorrow night.

JEN
(resentful)

Lucky you.

WILL

She said I could bring a guest. And I pick you.

JEN

What makes you think I'd want to go?

WILL

You're dying to. Admit it.

JEN

I might have other plans...

WILL

Break them!

JEN

You're awfully sure of yourself.

WILL

You can't tell me you're turning down an invitation to the president's house.

JEN

It's not from her. It's from you.

WILL

What's the difference?

JEN

A lot.

WILL

I don't get you.

JEN

I don't want to be a tag-along. I want to be invited of my own accord.

WILL

You're crazy...especially when you find out who else is coming.

JEN

Who?

WILL

Nah...You're obviously not interested.

JEN

Try me.

WILL

Does the name Dr. William H. Cosby sound familiar?

JEN

Bill Cosby! No way!

WILL

I'm serious.

JEN

I guess it's possible. He did give the commencement address here last year.

WILL

Are you coming or not?

JEN

Maybe I could rearrange things.

WILL

Great—I'll pick you up here at five.

THE WEEKLY SHOW
EPISODE ONE: "RICHARD LUSTER'S MEMBER"

Steve Lowery and Will Swaim
Irvine, CA

INT. NEWSROOM – DAY
MATT and TANYA are looking at a cover of the newspaper.

> MATT
> Doesn't look like a penis to me.

Idle chatter. Around the newsroom conference table, reporters begin to assemble. WILL enters.

> WILL
> All right, you communists. Once again, great job. The paper sparkles. It shines. It's completely devoid of transfats ... though it does have its usual share of fat trannys.

ANTHONY, looking at back of paper, nods knowingly at DAVE.

> DAVE
> (looking at paper, nodding)
> Love what he's done with the Adam's apple.

> WILL
> (paging through paper)
> Tanya: exquisite job on that groupie giving the Halos pitcher . . .

> TANYA
> Barnes.

> WILL
> (without looking up from the paper)

   . . . Barnes a blow job in the parking lot outside the stadium . . . and then, same night, Snarky...

> TANYA

Baines.

> WILL
> (without looking up from the paper)

. . . Baines—I get them confused—getting blown on stage at the New Orleans Bar in Fullerton. Two in a night.

> ANTHONY

This is the closest I've gotten to a blowjob in 18 months.

> TANYA

Honey, you've got to stop covering city council meetings and go where the action is. Start a band. Or join the Republican Central Committee.

> WILL

Nick: great job looking into the kid who got shot by the cops while he was holding a toy gun.

> STEVE

That the Huntington Beach kid?

> WILL

No, this is the Santa Ana kid. The Huntington Beach kid was holding a juice box ...

> STEVE

With intent.

WILL catches JON's eyes flitting back and forth, desperately hoping for recognition.

> WILL

And, of course, Jon's piece on the five things you should never say at a taco truck.

JON smiles.

                              STEVE

Number one: Hey, Taco Truck, you put on some
weight?

                              JON

No, no, it's …

Laughter drowns him out.

                              WILL

But I really want to discuss Steve's cover piece
about Richard Luster . . .

                            ANTHONY
                        (under his breath)

You said "Richard."

                              WILL

. . . specifically Mr. Luster's penis. Steve: Can you
give us the background? Luster's wife is filing for
divorce, right? And the court documents allege
that Mr. Luster—Orange County's biggest real
estate developer and most powerful figure in
conservative political causes—was romancing boys
on the side.

                              STEVE

Wasn't from the side.

                              WILL

That much we've already reported. Steve goes
on—brilliantly, here—to wonder whether that
private passion for gay sex and Luster's seemingly
contrary contributions to the campaigns of
extremely conservative political candidates finds its
release in the design of his many phallic buildings
around the city—specifically, Steve says, we find
that phallocentric obsession in the putt-putt
fountain at the Orange County Galleria shopping
center.

                              DAVE
                          (To Steve)

You said all that?

                              STEVE
                    Apparently I'm brilliant. Also, I use the word
                    "phallocentric."

WILL hands STEVE a copy of the paper, folded open to story, he points at
the intro.

                              WILL
                    Will you give us a dramatic reading?

STEVE grimaces slightly.

                              JON
                            (enthusiastically)
                    I'll do it!

JON picks up paper and reads.

                              JON
                    "I was willing to look past Richard Luster's penis
                    until it was suddenly staring me in the face:
                    outside his sprawling shopping and entertainment
                    complex, six, eight, maybe 10 feet high, thrusting
                    into the sky, rock-hard, tanned, encircled by
                    portals feeding a pool below into which children
                    dangled their unshod feet …"

Some laugh along with the reading.

                              WILL
                    This is what we do best. We're a tiny paper, with
                    a small staff, cowboys in Indian territory, and
                    people love us because we do what newspapers are
                    supposed to do. It's the reason the press is the only
                    industry mentioned in the Constitution.

                              MATT
                    And what does the Constitution say about calling
                    out a dude's taint?

                              WILL
                    That we're not afraid to take on the most powerful
                    real estate developer in Orange County…

TANYA

And our biggest advertiser...

WILL

... because it shows our readers we report what's
important in this county without fear or favor.

MATT

Also, that we have a deathwish.

TANYA

(Unselfconsciously adjusting her breasts)
I know what I'd do if someone wrote about my
penis . . .
(Turns to Will)
I'd sue.

WILL

For what?

TANYA

Libel. Defamation. Clear malice.

WILL

That's why you're not worth several billion
dollars and running the largest real estate firm in
California.

DAVE

But you have a fantastic penis.

WILL

First, Luster gets what we're about. Second, even if
he goes nuts, goes nuts and threatens legal action,
his guys won't let him sue because ...

TANYA

I don't think his projects look like genitalia.

WILL

That much is opinion, hyperbole. Therefore
protected speech. But my point is, there's this, the
nuclear option: If Luster sues us, the first thing our
attorneys do is go into discovery. They rape his
computers and his files digging for more evidence

to support our claims. We subpoena his top execs, his secretary, former aggrieved boyfriends . . . his bitter wife and offspring. We publish every thing we find. So, what's up for next week? Patty, keep the runlist. Nick?

NICK
(looking at the paper, absent-minded)
Something. Probably more dead kids with holes in 'em.

WILL
Tanya?

TANYA
(Sarcastic)
I dunno. Maybe a club this week?

WILL
Which one?

TANYA
(Sweetly)
How about one with dance music, coke and big-breasted girls?

WILL
Anthony?

ANTHONY
Himalaya Development wants to build a trash incinerator in a Santa Ana barrio.

WILL
G?

JON
I'm writing my food column about this great Mexican place that serves turtle soup.

WILL
Mock?

JON
Still in the shell. Real stuff. See, sea turtles are

protected, but these are farm-raised. Louisiana.
Shipped out here. Also . . .

                    WILL
          (turns to Patty, looks at what she's writing)
          Put him down for soup. And let's see . . . Scott?

Some STAFFERS make a show of searching for SCOTT under papers,
under the table.

                    WILL
          Anybody know where our investigative reporter is
          today?

                    STEVE
          I can never remember whether Thursday is his
          cloak or his dagger day.

                    WILL
          (Leaning over to check Patty's runlist)
          Who's next? Matt, whaddya got?

                    MATT
          Apparently the one story that doesn't threaten our
          revenue stream.

                    DAVE
          That's because 24-year-olds with drum machines
          don't buy ads.

                    TANYA
          My boyfriend's 38 and he has a drum machine.

                    WILL
                    (To Matt)
          We'll talk later.
                    (To all)
          Let's get to it.

STAFFERS exit in conversation. PATTY catches up to WILL.

                    PATTY
                    (To Will)
          Can we talk about deadlines? Stories are coming in
          late, and I'm getting slammed, and the production

department is …

WILL keeps walking.

> IN THE BACKGROUND, UNIDENTIFIED
> So is that the penis?

> SOMEONE ELSE
> I guess it's all penis.

INT. OFFICE HALLWAY – DAY
STEVE and WILL walking a hallway that connects the newsroom with
WILL's office.

> WILL
> Matt seemed especially bleak.

> STEVE
> Hard to see that through Tanya's envy.

> WILL
> She hasn't been on the cover in a while.

> STEVE
> Is that what the kids are calling being in a
> relationship with a 38-year-old dude with a drum
> machine?

> VOICE OFF-CAMERA
> There are a lot of jerks in the Bible.

> WILL
> (Stops, turns to speaker)
> Story.

> VOICE OFF-CAMERA
> What?

> WILL
> Jerks in the Bible. It's a great story. Write it.

STEVE and WILL continue walking.

                    STEVE
No. 1 jerk?

            VOICE OFF-CAMERA
God.

                    STEVE
Old Testament God.

                    WILL
Such a knob.

                    STEVE
Great name for a band: God Knob.

                    WILL
Drowns all of humanity, well, except Noah.

                    STEVE
Can you imagine the survivor's guilt?

                    WILL
And the mildew.

They stop to look into the production department where HEATHER has a
photo shoot going with an ASSISTANT in a ball gag and blindfold.

                    WILL
Great cover this week. Deliciously phallic.

                    HEATHER
That's how I like my phallics.

In the hall, outside production, Will's secretary OFELIA taps him on the
shoulder.

                    OFELIA
                    (Hushed)
Lacey's on hold for you.

                    WILL
How's he sound?

                    STEVE
Evil?

OFELIA
(To Will)
Where do you want him?

STEVE
Dangerous question.

WILL
Put him through to my desk, would you?

STEVE and WILL continue the walk.

STEVE
'Course, by the New Testament, totally new guy; very loving.

WILL
Well, he switches from killing everybody else to killing his own kid.

STEVE
Sure, but lovingly.

INT. BOHEMIAN COFFEEHOUSE -- DAY
TANYA and ANTHONY are getting coffee for three at the counter. They turn and walk gingerly to their table where DAVE is reading the paper.

DAVE
(Putting down paper)
You know, Tanya, this really is a good column.

TANYA
You sound surprised.

DAVE
No! It's great because it's not really about blow jobs.

ANTHONY
(crestfallen)
It's not?

DAVE
You've done for baseball what you've always done for the club scene.

                    ANTHONY
Both have organs.

                    TANYA
Music's better at the stadium.

                    DAVE
                 (still upbeat)
But apparently the sex is the same.

                    TANYA
                 (Hollow.)
This is getting old. I don't want to do clubs
anymore. Tired of guys asking if my boobs are
real.

DAVE's eyes flicker down once.

                    TANYA
I'm tired of dead-behind-the-eyes 25-year-old club
kids who think they're having a good time because
they paid a $50 cover and go [she raises her fist in
the air and screams] "Wooooooooooooo!"

                    OFF-CAMERA VOICE
                 (With real enthusiasm)
Wooooooooooooo!

                    TANYA
I'm not a kid anymore. I have a kid. We've all got
to grow up. We've got hooker ads in the back of
the paper. I'm writing about blowjobs. Steve's
suddenly an expert on the relationship between Le
Courbosier and gay sex?

TANYA waves the paper at DAVE.

                    TANYA
                 (adamant)
Do you really think this looks like a penis?

                    DAVE
Well, Will . . .

                              TANYA
                 Will needs to grow up.

INT. WILL'S OFFICE -- DAY

STEVE and WILL are looking out the floor-to-ceiling windows. We see
the tops of building and ample sky. WILL is gesturing at his own pelvis.

                              WILL
                      (Yelling, provocative)
                 Woooooooooo!

                             STEVE
                 They're up there?

                              WILL
                 Oh, they're out there. How's it going?

                             STEVE
                 My wife's unhappy.

                              WILL
                 Every American woman is unhappy. Why do you
                 think our biggest advertising category is mail-
                 order foreign brides.

                             STEVE
                 She's miserable. Says the kids don't love her and
                 the housekeeper's a slob and her employees are
                 jerks.

                              WILL
                 The tension between the domestic and work
                 spheres. Remember Foucault . . .

                             STEVE
                 (Incredulous)
                 I really don't want to hear about German
                 philosophers. And when she's not working, she's
                 working out all the time.

                              WILL
                 French.

STEVE

What?

WILL

Michel Foucault was French. There's this whole post-feminist conflict between work, body, home. We haven't resolved the legitimate achievements of feminism. And now, mark me, old man, unresolved, they're the leading killers of women in America.

STEVE

And sex.

WILL

How do you mean?

STEVE

My wife has a problem with our sex life.

WILL

What problem?

STEVE

Just once more in my life, I'd like to have sex.

WILL looks distracted.

STEVE
(Tortured, hesitates, stumbles)
I'm not saying I'm suicidal. But there are moments when I, I don't, I don't, are you checking your email?

WILL
(Lying)
No.

WILL stares at STEVE in a pose of perfect listening. The phone rings, jarring them both. Will leaps to it, picks up the phone--eyes still locked on STEVE.

WILL
(Impatiently, into the phone)

I'm still waiting. Put him through.

(To Steve)
You know what you have here, friend?

                    STEVE
No, no.

                    WILL
Story.

                    STEVE
I'm not writing about this. It's my life.

                    WILL
Ever heard of Marcel Proust?

                    STEVE
Ever heard of Rick Anderson?

                    WILL
Rick's story was great. Coming out gay; completely
revelatory.

                    STEVE
Especially to his wife. And his kid.

Phone rings. Incessant.

                    WILL
Won an award.

                    STEVE
Lives alone.

                    WILL
That's his next story: an examination of alienation
in America. "Bowling alone." The rise of social
networks on the Internet. Durkheim's concept of
anomie ...

STEVE gets up and starts walking out. WILL reaches for the ringing
phone, pauses.

                    WILL

(Shouting)
Great story! Everyone wants to know why your
wife won't have sex with you!

STEVE is already clear of the door.

                              WILL
              Can I get it by Wednesday?

Phone rings.

INT. NEWSROOM -- DAY
Phone ringing. ANTHONY, DAVE and TANYA walk back into newsroom.
Sound of phone ringing. We see SCOTT reach out to Tanya's desk and grab
her phone.

                             TANYA
                          (sotto voce)
              Never sit next to the investigative guy.

                             SCOTT
              Tanya Ramirez's desk. Tanya? She's...

SCOTT swivels around in his chair to check with TANYA. She signals that
she's not there.

                             SCOTT
              . . . not here. Can I take a message? Angels. Uh,
              huh. Pitcher denies it. Married.

                             SCOTT
              Well, if he's married, that makes it more likely he'd
              get a blowjob from a groupie in the . . .

                             SCOTT
              Right. Denies it. Got it. Number? So long.

SCOTT turns to Tanya, flourishes the piece of paper.

                             SCOTT
              Halos say the parking-lot oral never happened.

                             TANYA
              Oh, it happened.

75

                    SCOTT
        Pitcher denies it. Management wants you to
        produce the fillater or run a retraction.

TANYA simply stares at SCOTT.

                            SCOTT
                            (flat)
            It's you.

                            TANYA
                            (proud)
        And I'd do it again.

INT. WILL'S OFFICE - DAY
WILL looks out the window. Talking on the phone.

                    WILL
                        (enthusiastically)
        Michael!

                            (Pauses.)

        I'm glad you liked it.

                            (Pauses.)

        You didn't like it.

                            (Pauses.)

        You don't know what what is?

                            (Pauses.)

        "Taint." Well, it's a colloquialism for the spot on
        between the, um, rectum and the, um, the balls. Or
        the vagina. The genitalia of whatever. But it's . . . .

                            (Pauses.)

        Really just a metaphor for the space between two,
        you know, marginally repellant things, like vaginas
        and …

(Pauses.)

Uh, no, I'm not. And I believe the preferred
nomenclature is "gay."

(Pauses.)

Well, you're in New York.

(Pauses.)

Well, it makes a difference. Out here—anywhere,
really—Richard Luster is on the Forbes Top 10
wealthiest Americans every year. He's the biggest
developer in North America . . .

(Pauses.)

Yes, and his company is our biggest advertiser.

(Pauses.)

And he's a political player. A legitimate subject
of inquiry. Got billions of dollars, and just pours
millions into the campaigns of these Neanderthals
in the Republican party, these right-wing guys who
talk about family values and abortion and the evils
of gay marriage on camera--and then get popped
for meth possession in the presence of young boys.
And Luster himself is out there paying off these
boys to keep quiet, all over the . . . in some other
states. And all of this is in court documents, court
documents Steve has in his hands . . . .

(Pauses.)

Michael: Forget about taint. You're missing the
point.

(Pauses.)

No, Luster won't pull his ads.

(Pauses.)

Because It's all pro wrestling. He's a smart
businessman. He advertises with us because he
knows that stories like this bring readers, readers
who want to live in his homes and apartments. No
way he's going to pull his ad.

INT. SALES DEPARTMENT -- DAY
We catch PATTY in mid-conversation with drop-dead gorgeous sales rep
JEN. JEN isn't really interested in what PATTY is saying, and distractedly
searches the newsroom looking for STEVE.

> PATTY
> (Loudly, so that others may hear)
> . . . the cover was supposed to be about some band
> Matt likes, but then Will dumps this Steve story on
> me like Friday night because if Steve thinks it's
> funny then Will thinks it's funny . . .

> JEN
> Do you think it's funny?

> PATTY
> (oblivious)
> And then Will tells me he's got changes from the
> lawyers . . .

> JEN
> Lawyers?

> PATTY
> ... who just want to make sure everything's nailed
> down but Steve didn't do any of that.

> JEN
> What does Steve do? Are Will and Steve lovers?

> PATTY
> I'm not complaining because it's just like my job to put
> out the whole paper and make sure we don't get
> sued . . .

> JEN
> How about making sure we don't lose $200,000 in ads?
> We, I, lost the Luster account because of that story.
> Two-hundred grand.

                    PATTY
        ...and I'm here till like 10 o'clock Friday night because
        someone has to fact-check the story and lay it out.
                    JEN
        Not that Will and Steve would care. Do those guys
        ever think about anyone else? Are they Mormons?

JEN sees STEVE entering the office kitchen and takes off, leaving PATTY
talking to no one.

                    PATTY
        These things don't lay themselves out. Don't just
        pop out of the computer. And I'm here all day
        Saturday ...

INT. OFFICE KITCHEN -- DAY
STEVE is pouring a cup of coffee when JEN enters.

                    JEN
        Hi, Steve!

Startled, STEVE wheels dangerously around with the coffee pot.

                    STEVE
        (Searching for her name.)
        Heeeeeey . . .

                    JEN
        Jen.

                    STEVE
        I know. Jen. From . . .

                    JEN
        Advertising sales.

                    STEVE
        We love us the ads. Money. How're things
        over there?

CHILDREN'S/YOUNG ADULT FICTION WINNERS

1 Barbara Chamberlain
Aptos CA

2 Kelly Gibian
Jacksonville FL

3 David R. Davis
Fort Worth TX

4 Sara Matson
Carver MN

5 Nancy E. Walker
Traverse City MI

6 Lori Anastasia
North Attleboro MA

7 Kathleen Cherry
Kitimat BC Canada

8 Gay Seltzer
Sherman Oaks CA

9 Kathleen Palm
Woodburn IN

10 Barbara Lopuszynski
Langley WA

11 Becky Bartlett
Nazareth PA

12 Joan Eda Byrd
Phoenix AZ

13 Alicia Sheffield
Payson UT

14 Pamela Miller
Shepherdstown WV

15 Amy Finnegan
Highland UT

16 Brooke Frautschi
Ruckersville VA

17 Justin Rose
Corvallis OR

18 Bryanne Yearley
Simi Valley CA

19 Vicki J. Footer
Rockville MD

20 Gail Vannelli
Chagrin Falls OH

21 Janice Levy
Merrick NY

22 Rachel Aguilar
Green Bay WI

23 Cynthia Kozlowski
Fort Pierce FL

24 Lori Anastasia
North Attleboro MA

25 Michelle Mach
Fort Collins CO

26 Cindy Bennett
West Jordan UT

27 Bobbi Porter
Anchorage AK

28 William Thompson
Fremont CA

29 Terri Lynn Merritts
Nashville TN

30 Ellen L. Ramsey
Downingtown PA

31 Laura Heaney
Saint Lazare QU Canada

32 Tammy Bosch
Carstairs AB Canada

33 Gay Seltzer
Sherman Oaks CA

34 Elena Lelia Radulescu
Hackensack NJ

35 Hillary Yocum
Salem OH

36 Philip Ashworth
Pahrump NV

37 Neal Levin
Bloomfield Hills MI

38 Julie Teplitz
San Antonio TX

39 Lynne Higgins
Atascadero CA

40 Joanna Cherry
Pinellas Park FL

41 Donald Bonin
Madison MS

42 Donna McDine
Tappan NY

43 Tammy Bosch
Carstairs AB Canada

44 Carla J. Trabert
Columbia City IN

45 Colette Ballard
Bloomfield KY

46 Colette Ballard
Bloomfield KY

47 Shelley Arnfield
Port Alberni BC Canada

48 Brooke Frautschi
Ruckersville VA

49 Melanie R. Dundy
Wilsonville OR

50 Patti Meyers
Oak Lawn IL

51 Kathleen M. St. Claire
Menlo Park CA

52 Tracy Bilen
Troy MI

53 Kimberly Dana
Culver City CA

54 Sandra Gordon
Phoenix AZ

55 Jeffrey L. Urrutia
New Brunswick NJ

56 Linda Aschbrenner
Marshfield WI

57 JoAnn Early Macken
Shorewood WI

58 Rhonda S. Filipan
Stow OH

59 Kristin Enkvetchakul
Washington MO

60 Jane Nakatani
Tucson AZ

61 Sindy Thomas
Oakland CA

62 Rebecca Gail
Billings MT

63 Tony Brown
Greenville NC

64 Rita Hestand
Wylie TX

65 Donna McDine
Tappan NY

66 Marcia Corbino
Sarasota FL

67 Jhannet Marantonio
Alexandria VA

68 Jhannet Marantonio
Alexandria VA

69 Chad Douglas
Dunnellon FL

70 Andrew C McDonald
Palm Bay FL

71 Willa Holmes
Portland OR

72 Dean Eversole
Greenville OH

73 Tanya Spencer
Tehachapi CA

74 Catalina Claussen
Silver City NM

75 Jean York
Denver CO

76 Sherry Miller
Coloma MI

77 Della C. Jones
Houston TX

78 Ada and Nick Thipsingh
Saint Albans WV

79 Sarah M. Isaacson
Verona ND

80 Dana Harkins
Bellingham WA

81 Susan Alexander
Albany CA

82 Natalie C. Kegulian
Glendale CA

83 Kristen Bailey
Roseburg OR

84 Teeka Thompson
Salem OR

85 Barbara Fitz Vroman
Hancock WI

86 Deanna Le
Aurora CO

87 Barbara J. Bina
Puyallup WA

88 Peggy Raposa
Coventry RI

89 Marc Van Lent
Salt Lake City UT

90 Kathy Bjornestad
Sundance WY

91 Kjersten Hayes
Bellingham WA

92 Alicia McHugh
Sterling MA

93 Ian Sherman
Chappaqua NY

94 Cindy Christian Rogers
Maple Grove MN

95 James Marquardt
Sag Harbor NY

96 Sally Hirst
Kenosha WI

97 Lorna Foreman
Cornwall ON Canada

98 Bettye McHenry
Kearney MO

99 Holly Ireland
Cardiff United Kingdom

100 Tom Cantillon
Chatham NJ

FEATURE ARTICLE WINNERS

1 Renee Roberson
Huntersville NC
2 Suzanne Johnson
Auburn AL
3 Lance Wills
North Charleston SC
4 Jan Sherbin
5 Anna B. Billingsley
Fredericksburg VA
6 Vocki Soulé
7 Brian Trent
Prospect CT
8 Ruth Tick
Venice FL
9 Paige Stringer
10 Richard Muti
Ramsey NJ
11 John Moir
Santa Cruz CA
12 Gail Koger
Glendale AZ
13 Wanda Hennig
Oakland CA
14 Sherrie Dulworth
Mt. Kisco NY
15 Nancy Hoag
Bozeman MT
16 Christa Gala
Apex NC
17 Cynthia Lewis
Davidson NC
18 Lisa Tarrants
Camden NC
19 Charles Green
Annapolis MD
20 Paula Surrey
Auburn ME
21 Amy Souza
Arlington VA
22 Suzanne Johnson
Auburn AL
23 Ann Hyman
Burbank CA
24 Russell W. Eastlack
St. George UT
25 Kim A. O'Connell
Arlington VA
26 Jeanette A. Fratto
Laguna Niguel CA
27 Aneeta Brown
Washington MO
28 Paula Surrey
Auburn ME
29 Roger White
Austin TX
30 Bill J. Harrison
Mesa AZ
31 Russell W. Eastlack
St. George UT
32 Christy Heitger
Bloomington IN
33 Mark E. Daugherty
Staunton VA
34 Calvin Sun
Paoli PA
35 Russell W. Eastlack
St. George UT
36 Victor Englebert
Allentown PA

37 Dan Tomasulo
Sea Girt NJ
38 Richard Hicks
Cardiff By The Sea CA
39 Robin Hastings
Jefferson City MO
40 Sherrie Bourg Carter
Fort Lauderdale FL
41 Jane Baskin
Tijeras NM
42 Paschal Young
East Boothbay ME
43 Paula Surrey
Auburn ME
44 Sarah Stover
Huachuca City AZ
45 Trish Scozzari
Butte MT
46 Calvin Sun
Paoli PA
47 Darlene Kapur
Roseville CA
48 Susan K. Maciak
Jenison MI
49 Christy Heitger
Bloomington IN
50 Dennis G. Sellers
Bloomington IN
51 Angela Cannon
Prattsburgh NY
52 Kay Daly
Chicago IL
53 Paul Vachon
Huntington Woods MI
54 Eva Ditler
Coronado CA
55 Cathy Cassinos-Carr
Sacramento CA
56 Monica Arlene Gold
Massapequa NY
57 Sylvia Forbes
Fayette MO
58 Michelle Smith, MD
Monterey CA
59 Mary Owen
Salem OR
60 Andy Aligne
Rochester NY
61 Karen Hutto
Dacula GA
62 Sarah Asp Olson
Statesboro GA
63 Mary Ann DeSantis
Lady Lake FL
64 Becky Aaronson
Santa Barbara CA
65 Brent Green
Denver CO
66 Karen Hutto
Dacula GA
67 Robin Clifford Wood
Hampden ME
68 Jennifer Della'Zanna
Columbia MD
69 Jeannette Monahan
Glendale AZ
70 Allan C. Stover
The Villages FL

71 Mary Ann DeSantis
Lady Lake FL
72 Richard Muti
Ramsey NJ
73 Rita Connelly
Tucson AZ
74 Barbara Neal Varma
Lake Forest CA
75 Christy Heitger
Bloomington IN
76 Karen Fiordaliso
Blackwood NJ
77 Cathy Cassinos-Carr
Sacramento CA
78 Dayle Allen Shockley
Spring TX
79 Victor Englebert
Allentown PA
80 Mary Ann DeSantis
Lady Lake FL
81 Dan Tomasulo
Sea Girt NJ
82 Charles Green
Annapolis MD
83 Robert Decker
Moreno Valley CA
84 Becky Aaronson
Santa Barbara CA
85 Bryna Kranzler
La Jolla CA
86 Melissa Crytzer Fry
Mammoth AZ
87 Nancy Marano
Albuquerque NM
88 Pat Stockett Johnston
Temple City CA
89 Fran B. Reed
Hilton Head SC
90 Maggie Ownbey
Burbank CA
91 Sylvia Forbes
Fayette MO
92 Geri Hoekzema
Vancouver WA
93 Calvin Sun
Paoli PA
94 Trish Scozzari
Butte MT
95 Melissa Crytzer Fry
Mammoth AZ
96 Nic Brown
Lexington KY
97 Diane Lebow
San Francisco CA
98 Pam Windsor
Louisville KY
99 Alice L. Geroge
Philadelphia PA
100 Nancy Churchill
Princeton IL

GENRE SHORT STORY WINNERS

1 **Mart Shaughnessy**
   Perris CA
2 **Amanda Sigquefield**
   Olive Branch MS
3 **Alex Sinclair**
   Stratford CT
4 **Michael Fourman**
   Covington GA
5 **Shelia Romano**
   Elk Grove CA
6 **Gerry Griffiths**
   San Jose CA
7 **Dawn Boeder Johnson**
   Stillman Valley IL
8 **Tialena Elliott**
   Jamaica NY
9 **Ben R. Philibert**
   Saint Louis MO
10 **Robert Norton**
   Portland OR
11 **Katy Kellogg**
   Las Vegas NV
12 **Trish Field**
   San Clemente CA
13 **Matthew Maybray**
   Drexel Hill PA
14 **Hope R. Gillette**
   Binghamton NY
15 **Jeff McCormick**
   Lakeland FL
16 **H.M. Snow**
   Minneapolis MN
17 **Aaron Patterson**
   Rocky River OH
18 **James McGowan**
   Omaha NE
19 **Ronald Sitarski**
   Fort Lauderdale FL
20 **Matthew Maybray**
   Drexel Hill PA
21 **Richard Goodman**
   Boone NC
22 **James Greer**
   Commerce City CO
23 **Robert S. Kidd**
   North Vancouver BC Canada
24 **Alicia Stankay**
   Ambridge PA
25 **Rachel Kyle**
   Lumberport WV
26 **Jen Colbert**
   Redford MI
27 **Jon Ripslinger**
   Davenport IA
28 **David M. Thomas**
   Monterey CA
29 **Brian Trent**
   Prospect CT
30 **Steve Dimeo**
   Hillsboro OR
31 **M. Grace Matthews**
   Albany NY
32 **Chris Alesso**
   Pleasanton CA
33 **Fran M. McGovern**
   Apache Junction AZ
34 **Katie Pinelli**
   The Woodlands TX

35 **David M. Thomas**
   Monterey CA
36 **Jason Miller**
   Pittsburgh PA
37 **Christopher Hyatt**
   Florence KY
38 **Dan Tomasulo**
   Sea Girt NJ
39 **Linda Spoerner**
   Poway CA
40 **Steven Cormey**
   Medford MA
41 **Steven White**
   Shoreline WA
42 **Rochelle Weidner**
   Kaneohe HI
43 **J. Steven Fleming**
   Phoenix AZ
44 **Tim J. Rocheford Jr.**
   Zimmerman MN
45 **Laurie Miles**
   Placentia CA
46 **Sasha d'Or**
   Pinckney MI
47 **Diana Gudrian**
   Easton PA
48 **J. Patrick Geraghty**
   Bayonne NJ
49 **Alisa Kester**
   Mount Vernon WA
50 **Ruth Welburn**
   Sidney BC Canada
51 **Joanna R. Smith**
   Cave Creek AZ
52 **M. Grace Matthews**
   Albany NY
53 **D. J. Bianca**
   Pompton Plains NJ
54 **Victoria Ohlin**
   Akron OH
55 **Alan Naditz**
   Sacramento CA
56 **Michael Pirillo**
   Rome NY
57 **John Naylor**
   Monroeville AL
58 **Laurie Perkins**
   Needham MA
59 **Bruce Graham**
   Winter Park FL
60 **Mark E. Daugherty**
   Staunton VA
61 **Brenda L. Witcher**
   Denison TX
62 **Hilary Tomasek**
   Cookville TX
63 **Lisa Fish**
   Bloomington IN
64 **Maureen Callan Fisher**
   Eden Prairie MN
65 **Kathy Dowell**
   Vidor TX
66 **Ebony Mathis-Modlin**
   Westchester CA
67 **Christian Triola**
   Norton OH
68 **Laurie Perkins**
   Needham MA

69 **Hamilton Waymire**
   Irvine CA
70 **Ruth Welburn**
   Sidney BC Canada
71 **John J. White**
   Merritt Island FL
72 **Brian Trent**
   Prospect CT
73 **Benjamin H. Foreman**
   Port Orange FL
74 **Steve Pantazis**
   Carlsbad CA
75 **James C. Devine**
   El Paso TX
76 **W. E. Mueller**
   Chesterfield MO
77 **Gabriela Santin**
   Broken Arrow OK
78 **Gerald Griffiths**
   San Jose CA
79 **Bernie Bourdeau**
   Lakeland FL
80 **Debbie Gillette**
   Fort Worth TX
81 **Jennifer Porter**
   Ortonville MI
82 **Hunter Goddard**
   Englewood CO
83 **Steven A. Conness**
   Ottawa IL
84 **D.B. Jacobson**
   Sewell NJ
85 **Melanie Bacon**
   Waxhaw NC
86 **Richard Murphy**
   San Augustine TX
87 **Silvia Nena**
   San Pedro CA
88 **Patricia Bowman-Stein Gyulai**
   North Hollywood CA
89 **Rebecca Embrich**
   Simi Valley CA
90 **Ashley B. Summers**
   Eureka Springs AR
91 **W. E. Mueller**
   Chesterfield MO
92 **Sandra Buford**
   Deatsville AL
93 **Robbb Lightfoot**
   Palo Cedro CA
94 **Dada Nabhaniilananda**
   Los Altos Hills CA
95 **Mirja Salminen**
   Bellingham WA
96 **William Scar**
   Rancho Palos Verdes CA
97 **Joseph W. Porter**
   Venice FL
98 **Christina Chandler**
   Manahawkin NJ
99 **Chloe Ryan Winston**
   Redding CA
100 **Daniel Schuler**
   Mobile AL

INSPIRATIONAL WRITING WINNERS

1 Courtney Gainer
  Grand Island FL
2 Elisha Wagman
  Reston VA
3 Susan Winzelberg
  Toms River NJ
4 Beth Woodard
  Bloomington IL
5 Lyn G. Brakeman
  Gloucester MA
6 Alison Hodgson
  Ada MI
7 Debra Easterling
  Sanford FL
8 Susan M. Watkins
  Woodstock GA
9 Jocelyn Krieger
  Boca Raton FL
10 Jon McCauley
11 Linda Capelli Pierce
  Long Beach CA
12 Thomas Heyd
  Becker MN
13 Dawn Baldwin
  Lewisburg WV
14 Tami Herzer-Absi
  Dayton OH
15 Karen Frascona
  Holliston MA
16 John Hinch
  Centurion South Africa
17 Carol Green
  Walnut Creek CA
18 Lucille C. Carlson
  Forest Lake MN
19 Donna
  Concord NH
20 Lisa Shults
  Lincolnton NC
21 Karen A. Ellis
  Encinitas CA
22 Diana DeSpain
  Sun Prairie WI
23 Gloria Shirr
  West Hills CA
24 Joshua Demke
  Syracuse NY
25 Cindi Degeyter
  Bridge City TX
26 Chris Fraser
  Toronto ON Canada
27 Cheri Moser-Coomer
  Seymour IN
28 Diane Schultz
  Belleville IL
29 Sherri Gragg
  Franklin TN
30 Karen Pickett-Woodland
  Roswell GA
31 Pamela Maiato
  Natick MA
32 Melanie Moore
  Elizabethton TN
33 Wendy Kirkby
  Concord MI
34 Gerald Osterberg
  Garden City NY

35 Jan O'Banion Pender
  Florence SC
36 Donna Carter
  Huntsville AL
37 Christina Walters
  Akron OH
38 Elizabeth MacDonald Burrows
  Seattle WA
39 Vince Hodgins
  Kissimmee FL
40 Robert Robeson
  Lincoln NE
41 Terry Wolfe
  Colorado Springs CO
42 Gail Jenner
  Etna CA
43 Kathryn Nielson
  Peoria IL
44 Louy Castonguay
  West Farmington ME
45 Pamela Kaye Klopfenstein
  Huber Heights OH
46 Rick Martin
  Charlottesville VA
47 Brian Sweeney
  Bethany OK
48 Dorothy Searing
  Tarpon Springs FL
49 Katherine Bradley
  Keller TX
50 Janice Coy
  San Diego CA
51 Judi Roberts
  Springville IN
52 Ruth Clark
  Mukilteo WA
53 Ruth Clark
  Mukilteo WA
54 Beverly Rivera Davis
  Hurley NY
55 Denise Kay
  Coram NY
56 M. J. Smith
  Scottsdale AZ
57 Joanne K. Hill
  South Bend IN
58 Brenda Silverhand
  Corning NY
59 Lisa Dye
  Westfield IN
60 Marriana Martinez
  Houston TX
61 Rhonda Larson
  Soldotna AK
62 Sara McLaughlin
  Lubbock TX
63 Nancy Hoag
  Bozeman MT
64 James B. Wood
  Fountainville PA
65 Reg Ivory
  Johnson City TN
66 David J Nelson
  Kenner LA
67 Carol Shaw
  Garland TX
68 Bradley C. Skilton
  Orlando FL

69 Phil Gale
  Duncan BC Canada
70 Swarnali Ahmed
  London United Kingdom
71 Robynn Reilly
  Clovis CA
72 Robynn Reilly
  Clovis CA
73 Sandra Ramirez
  Cleveland OH
74 Judy Crowder
  Morehead City NC
75 Veronica Breen Hogle
  Buffalo NY
76 Tess Almendarez Lojacono
  East Aurora NY
77 Kevin Fobbs
  Willis MI
78 Cheryl A. Knight
  Milton WA
79 Cheryl B. Lemine
  Jacksonville FL
80 M. P. Liebchen
  Altavista VA
81 Dale Worcester
  Central City PA
82 Sally Paradysz
  Coopersburg PA
83 LaRae Black
  Blanding UT
84 H. Michael Brooks
  Greensboro NC
85 Connie Lounsbury
  Monticello MN
86 Amy L. Turek
  Wheaton IL
87 John P. Dick
  Midland MI
88 Kaye Khalsa
  Franklin MA
89 Janis Hutchinson
  Everett WA
90 Maggie Weidner
  Columbus OH
91 Dorothy "Candace" Rice
  Rathdrum ID
92 Matthew Elvin Bridges
  Clovis CA
93 Carol A. Cichella
  Rockford IL
94 Brad McCloud
  Newport News VA
95 Jackie Strange
  Bogalusa LA
96 Anne Meyer
  Indianapolis IN
97 Elaine P. Gordon
  Brentwood TN
98 Dixie Pettit
  Ramona CA
99 Christine A. Malkemes
  Kissimmee FL
100 Aleada T. Nicholson
  Mobile AL

MAINSTREAM/LITERARY SHORT STORY WINNERS

1 **Yvette Whitaker**
Cody WY

2 **Tim Rocheford, Jr.**
Zimmerman MN

3 **Marilyn Mansfield**
Potomac MD

4 **Yvette Whitaker**
Cody WY

5 **Sharon Svesnik**
Jacksonburg WV

6 **Heather Ricks**
Lithonia GA

7 **Donna Welch Jones**
Tahlequah OK

8 **Nancy Jean Carrigan**
Warrenville IL

9 **Anna Lefler**
Santa Monica CA

10 **Jim Fant**
Dallas TX

11 **Patsy Pittman**
Vienna WV

12 **Dorothy McMillan**
Riverside CA

13 **Hiley Ward**
Warrington PA

14 **Zachary Kyle McLendon**
Many LA

15 **Susan Alexander**
Albany CA

16 **Jessica Tedrick**
Hamilton OH

17 **Consuela Golden**
Hartsdale NY

18 **Richard C. Johnston**
Grove City OH

19 **Linda Smith**
San Mateo CA

20 **Paul Coleman**
Wappingers Falls NY

21 **John Cusack**
Isle Of Palms SC

22 **Jennifer Kuntz**
Norfolk VA

23 **Gerald A. Winter**
Whiting NJ

24 **Judy Bowen**
Millersville MD

25 **Gregory Frye**
Athens Greece

26 **Dorinda Ohnstad**
Hanford CA

27 **Michael Terry**
Honolulu HI

28 **Cassondra Windwalker**
Fort Collins CO

29 **Justine Mazin**
Toronto ON Canada

30 **Ara Corrigan**
Davenport IA

31 **Valerie Gilford**
Bronx NY

32 **Pat Dunnigan**
Riverside IL

33 **Sonia Suedfeld**
Langley BC Canada

34 **Arlene L. Walker**
Cerritos CA

35 **Paul Schultz**
Madison WI

36 **Bonnie Faye Dunn**
Healdsburg CA

37 **Ali Hajighafouri**
Concord CA

38 **Carol Wobig**
Milwaukee WI

39 **Hannah Langley**
Valencia CA

40 **Lori Otto**
Dallas TX

41 **Charlie M. Clint**
Portland OR

42 **Patsy E. Pittman**
Vienna WV

43 **Brian Mullally**
Coburg ON Canada

44 **Gerene Reid**
Bellingham WA

45 **Gale Whittington**
Wetumka OK

46 **Ramona Scarborough**
Salem OR

47 **Todd Reppert**
New York NY

48 **Florita Bradford**
Houston TX

49 **Kathie Gavel**
Crozet VA

50 **Yvonne Nelson Perry**
Bonita CA

51 **Lynda A. Babcock**
Glastonbury CT

52 **Casi Butts**
Pleasant Prairie WI

53 **May Allen**
Toronto ON Canada

54 **Mary Kennedy**
Beverly Hills FL

55 **Robert Sweeten**
Seneca MO

56 **Caitlin Woodcock**
Guelph ON Canada

57 **Stephen J. Ranson**
Manahawkin NJ

58 **Terri Laurent**
Grayling MI

59 **Ryan King**
Portland OR

60 **Debbie Cannizzaro**
Mandeville LA

61 **Christopher Hyatt**
Florence KY

62 **Andrew Zembles**
Corona Del Mar CA

63 **Christy Lynne Trotter**
Pontiac IL

64 **Shelia Sherrill**
Chatsworth GA

65 **Mike Ghirardelli**
Parker CO

66 **Daniel Peters**
Lewistown PA

67 **Valerie Norris**
Simpsonville SC

68 **Megan H. Wright**
Gaithersburg MD

69 **Suzannah Bowser**
Arcata CA

70 **Aimee Dansereau**
San Diego CA

71 **Jonathan Littlefield**
Somersworth NH

72 **Robert Sweeten**
Seneca MO

73 **Jimmy Pack Jr**
Philadelphia PA

74 **Jeanette A. Fratto**
Laguna Niguel CA

75 **Stefanie Kramer**
Earling IA

76 **Charles Bilderback**
Michigan City IN

77 **Tanya Babcock**
Wayland NY

78 **Oswald Angulo**
Gainesville FL

79 **Sabrina Escalante**
San Fernando CA

80 **Mary Ingmire**
Franklin TN

81 **Desiree McClain**
Harrisburg NC

82 **Benjamin Martinson**
Vincennes IN

83 **Robin Favello**
New Haven CT

84 **Stan Sveen**
Falcon Heights MN

85 **Stephen J. Ranson**
Manahawkin NJ

86 **Kim Pierce**
Pendleton IN

87 **Karen Robiscoe**
Santa Barbara CA

88 **Carolyn P.C. Martin**
Dallas TX

89 **Kenny Smith**
Edmond OK

90 **Angela R. Sherwood**
Kailua Kona HI

91 **Robert Godfrey**
Glen Allen VA

92 **Robin Favello**
New Haven CT

93 **Beverly Whitehead**
De Funiak Springs FL

94 **Camelia Townsend**
Great Falls VA

95 **Leslie Rodd**
San Francisco CA

96 **Frank Maciel**
Los Angeles CA

97 **Ray Abernathy**
Washington DC

98 **Nicole Rosner**
Pasadena TX

99 **Casi Butts**
Pleasant Prairie WI

100 **Alvaro de Araujo**
Dallas TX

MEMOIR/PERSONAL ESSAY WINNERS

1 Karen Z. Duffy
Ventnor NJ

2 Stephen P. Koch
Montgomery TX

3 Sandra L. Staton-Taiwo
York PA

4 Denise Walsh Brown
Canton OH

5 Ebony Adomanis
Albuquerque NM

6 Marcelline Burns
Oxnard CA

7 Jennifer Scharf
Boston MA

8 Linda Aschbrenner
Marshfield WI

9 Eva Ditler
Coronado CA

10 Kathleen M. Long
Beaver OR

11 Dori Gillam
Seattle WA

12 Rachel Kuhnle
Honey Creek IA

13 Mark Abellera
New York NY

14 Judy Belsky
Seattle WA

15 Barbara Pritchard
Las Vegas NV

16 Jerry Kaufmann
Parma Heights OH

17 Suzanne Handler
Greenwood Village CO

18 Joel Eckstein
Los Angeles CA

19 Susan Williamson
Rural Hall NC

20 Christopher Fahy
Thomaston ME

21 Sandra Lampella
Portland OR

22 Noelle Johnson
House Springs MO

23 Elizabeth Krakow
Corte Madera CA

24 Marcia J. Sargent
Laguna Beach CA

25 S. Belle Karper
Calabasas CA

26 Robynn Reilly
Clovis CA

27 Judy Belsky
Seattle WA

28 Ralph Ryan
Redding CA

29 Maria Feldman
Chicago IL

30 Deb Farrow
East Haddam CT

31 Alan Olifson
Sherman Oaks CA

32 Margaret Holeman
Hope AK

33 Veronica Sullivan
Old Bridge NJ

34 Lisa-marie Fusco
Brandon FL

35 Marcia Moston
Taylors SC

36 Barbara Chamberlain
Aptos CA

37 Dolores Runyon
Dallas TX

38 Dan Tomasulo
Sea Girt NJ

39 Lan Roberts
San Jose CA

40 Stanley M. Weintraub
St. Augustine FL

41 Roberta Miles
Chicago IL

42 Deb Lehman
Fanwood NJ

43 Taine Watkins
Bloomington IN

44 Mary K. Hull
Las Vegas NV

45 Alice Grant Bingner
Ann Arbor MI

46 Tharin Schwinefus
Iowa City IA

47 Becky Browder
Jacksonville AL

48 Jessica DeLandra
West Haven CT

49 Patrick Caneday
Burbank CA

50 Constance Hoffman
Burke SD

51 Nancy Ryan
Seabeck WA

52 Saara Dutton
New York NY

53 Phil Goldman
Warwick RI

54 Alexandra Pecci
Plaistow NH

55 Ruth Tick
Venice FL

56 Sharon Rea
Bellevue NE

57 Lois Cowan
Marathon FL

58 Candy Farlow
Quinby VA

59 Leah Koch Sower
Marion IN

60 Brit Williams
Austin TX

61 Thomas M. Davis
Huntington Station NY

62 Judy Ross
Los Angeles CA

63 Dan Bolchoz
Williamsburg VA

64 Brenda Watterson
Algonquin IL

65 Rachael Sokolowski
Truro MA

66 Sarah Yonder
Saginaw MI

67 Rosemarie Chaney
Massillon OH

68 Jessica Soleil
Portland OR

69 Melissa Cook
Spanaway WA

70 Pat Tyler
Cotati CA

71 Lisa A. Martin
Burbank CA

72 Scarlett L. Mayfield
Clarksville TN

73 Carolyn McGovern
Manalapan NJ

74 Kathryn Mallinger
Roanoke VA

75 Julie Curtis
Bethel CT

76 Marcia Kaplan
Sunnyvale CA

77 Robin Whitson-O'Flinn
Silt CO

78 Connie Vaughn
Cincinnati OH

79 Corinne Rumley
Baton Rouge LA

80 Nikki Tiani
Irwin PA

81 James M. Doumas
Port Orange FL

82 Lisa-marie Fusco
Brandon FL

83 Kimberly K. Schwartz
Burr Oak MI

84 Roberta Miles
Chicago IL

85 Mary E. Spear
Dallas TX

86 Nancy Corbett
Monroe WA

87 Rob Smythe
Burlington ON Canada

88 Michelle Weidenbenner
Warsaw IN

89 B. H. Amok
Palm Harbor FL

90 E. Cluff Elliott
Farmington NM

91 David Bates
Hollywood FL

92 Edward Haag
Greensboro NC

93 Michelle Sangiovanni
Huntington Station NY

94 Bill Riddle
Odessa FL

95 Martha Whitfield
Dearborn MI

96 Eileen P. Duggan
Saint Louis MO

97 Byron Browne
Austin TX

98 Stephen J. Ranson
Manahawkin NJ

99 Todd Townsend
Hudsonville MI

100 Nicole Hayes
Chadstone VIC Australia

NON-RHYMING POETRY WINNERS

1 **Norma Laughter**
Rutherfordton NC

2 **Maria Ercilla**
Los Angeles CA

3 **Cappy Love Hanson**
Douglas AZ

4 **Claire Hsu Accomando**
Bonita CA

5 **Sandra Louise Staton-Taiwo**
York PA

6 **John K. Rutenberg**
Myrtle Beach SC

7 **Juanita Torrence-Thompson**
Flushing NY

8 **Dawn Boeder Johnson**
Stillman Valley IL

9 **Marla Alupoaicei**
Frisco TX

10 **Marsha Bush**
Cedarville OH

11 **N. Harvey**
Bigfork MT

12 **William F. Bellais**
Chillicothe MO

13 **Hazel Winter**
Sydney Australia

14 **Patricia Corcoran**
New Milford CT

15 **Janice Cutbush**
Ballston Spa NY

16 **Arturo Cantu Hernandez**
San Antonio TX

17 **Sue C. Foster**
Lewistown MT

18 **Sue C. Foster**
Lewistown MT

19 **Robert Chute**
London ON Canada

20 **Maria Ercilla**
Los Angeles CA

21 **Debora Bray**
Lincoln NE

22 **R. H. Peat**
Auburn CA

23 **Elizabeth Y. Porter**
Eminence MO

24 **Maria Ercilla**
Los Angeles CA

25 **Sheila A. Murphy**
Portland CT

26 **Barbara Kiley**
Port Saint Lucie FL

27 **Rohan Alexander Rowe**
Lawrenceville GA

28 **Khaled KE Mahmoud**
London ON Canada

29 **Khaled KE Mahmoud**
London ON Canada

30 **Carol Wills**
Durham NC

31 **Cheyene L. Garwood**
Encino CA

32 **Sara McNulty**
Beaverton OR

33 **Julia Tatsch**
South Dennis MA

34 **Barbara L. McNinch**
Rocky Point NC

35 **Albert Russo**
Paris France

36 **Anni Gibson**
Cincinnati OH

37 **Anni Gibson**
Cincinnati OH

38 **Anni Gibson**
Cincinnati OH

39 **Becky Haigler**
Shreveport LA

40 **Patryk Zielonka**
Cranford NJ

41 **Gail Israel**
Los Angeles CA

42 **Gail Israel**
Los Angeles CA

43 **Jennifer A. Honaker**
Miami FL

44 **Angela Weaver**
Omaha NE

45 **Suellen Wedmore**
Rockport MA

46 **Christine M. Quirk**
Clinton MA

47 **Cathy Conger**
Wisconsin Rapids WI

48 **Brian Timmerman**
Canoga Park CA

49 **Dorothy Fulton-Stevens**
Abington PA

50 **Katherine Hauswirth**
Deep River CT

51 **Nina Soifer**
Northfield NJ

52 **Marilyn J. Humm**
Fairfax VA

53 **Chuck Warren**
Grandville MI

54 **Michael Thio**
San Diego CA

55 **Nicole Foltin**
Bethlehem PA

56 **Ziggy Donovan**
San Diego CA

57 **Jessica Harris**
Hiram GA

58 **Kendall Martin**
Richmond VA

59 **Cynthia Lukas**
Santa Fe NM

60 **Tom K. Wagner**
Phoenix AZ

61 **Denise Parent**
Milford CT

62 **Marie K. Wood**
Sun City Center FL

63 **R. F. Sedlack**
Sarasota FL

64 **Gini McCainWest**
St. Paul MN

65 **Tanya Wallace**
Milford CT

66 **Louis G. Redka**
Bridgeton NJ

67 **Steve Barfield**
West Palm Beach FL

68 **Del Corey**
Macomb MI

69 **Anne-Marie Legan**
Herrin IL

70 **Anne-Marie Legan**
Herrin IL

71 **Anne-Marie Legan**
Herrin IL

72 **Sara A. Harris**
Eureka MO

73 **Colleen Clancy Hansen**
Helena MT

74 **Nancy Jean Carrigan**
Warrenville IL

75 **Juanita Torrence-Thompson**
Flushing NY

76 **Juanita Torrence-Thompson**
Flushing NY

77 **Julie K. Everett**
Milwaukee WI

78 **Debora J. MacLean**
Chichester NH

79 **Debora J. MacLean**
Chichester NH

80 **Debora J. MacLean**
Chichester NH

81 **Tracy Lord**
Hope ME

82 **Gladys L. Henderson**
Nesconset NY

83 **Gladys L. Henderson**
Nesconset NY

84 **William F. Mitten**
Manchester NH

85 **Calder Lowe**
Columbia CA

86 **Calder Lowe**
Columbia CA

87 **Jean Youkers**
Hockessin DE

88 **Marla Alupoaicei**
Frisco TX

89 **Marla Alupoaicei**
Frisco TX

90 **Lori Van Pelt**
Saratoga WY

91 **Steve Barfield**
West Palm Beach FL

92 **Charles S. Rogers**
Brattleboro VT

93 **Marianne Y. Ray**
Kent WA

94 **Tammy L. Beevers**
Belton TX

95 **Margaret Schiller**
Greendell NJ

96 **Margaret Schiller**
Greendell NJ

97 **Debora J. MacLean**
Chichester NH

98 **Roger Crai**
Ashtabula OH

99 **Carol L. Vieira**
Parker CO

100 **David M. Thomas**
Monterey CA

RHYMING POETRY WINNERS

1   Marla Alupoaicei
    Frisco TX
2   Atar Hadari
    Hebden Bridge United Kingdom
3   Melissa Cannon
    Nashville TN
4   Melissa Cannon
    Nashville TN
5   Marla Alupoaicei
    Frisco TX
6   Ellen Godrey
    Foxboro MA
7   Anna Amatuzio
    New York NY
8   Dorothy Weems
    Huntsville AL
9   Valma M. Bartlett
    Oak Harbor WA
10   Robert Daseler
    Sacramento CA
11   Robert Daseler
    Sacramento CA
12   Herb Wahlsteen
    Farmingville NY
13   Herb Wahlsteen
    Farmingville NY
14   Marla Alupoaicei
    Frisco TX
15   Kristi Williams
    Lauderhill FL
16   James Waverly
    South Orange NJ
17   Dennis Mahagin
    Kennewick WA
18   L.A. Shively
    San Antonio TX
19   JLS Peck
    San Rafael CA
20   Jennifer Toon
    Houston TX
21   Linda Aschbrenner
    Marshfield WI
22   Marla Alupoaicei
    Frisco TX
23   Robert Daseler
    Sacramento CA
24   Robert Daseler
    Sacramento CA
25   Robert Daseler
    Sacramento CA
26   Robert Daseler
    Sacramento CA
27   Robert Daseler
    Sacramento CA
28   Robert Daseler
    Sacramento CA
29   Robert Daseler
    Sacramento CA
30   Herb Wahlsteen
    Farmingville NY
31   Herb Wahlsteen
    Farmingville NY
32   Herb Wahlsteen
    Farmingville NY
33   Herb Wahlsteen
    Farmingville NY
34   Herb Wahlsteen
    Farmingville NY

35   Herb Wahlsteen
    Farmingville NY
36   Herb Wahlsteen
    Farmingville NY
37   Melissa Cannon
    Nashville TN
38   David M. Thomas
    Monterey CA
39   John Bercaw
    Aurora IL
40   Mel Shock
    Wichita KS
41   David M McComas
    Champaign IL
42   Michelle Perez
    Secaucus NJ
43   Michelle Perez
    Secaucus NJ
44   Janet Ireland Trail
    Greensboro NC
45   Elizabeth Y. Porter
    Eminence MO
46   William A. Holt
    Fort Worth TX
47   Elizabeth Miravalle
    Clearlake Oaks CA
48   Katherine Edgren
    Dexter MI
49   Anita D. Loche
    Oakland CA
50   Linda Gayle O'Hern
    Oklahoma City OK
51   J. A. A. Wilkins
    Knoxville TN
52   Donna Penrice
    Erin ON Canada
53   Thomas Fullmer
    Salt Lake City UT
54   Barbara DuBois
    Socorro NM
55   David M. Thomas
    Monterey CA
56   Dorothy Lamar
    Woodbury NJ
57   Rex B. Valentine
    Elma WA
58   Robert Chute
    London ON Canada
59   Tara Lynn Johnson
    Quesnel BC Canada
60   Janice Watrous
    Knoxville TN
61   Ara Hagopian
    North Chelmsford MA
62   Sherwin Kaufman
    New York NY
63   Cara Nusinov
    Coconut Grove FL
64   Barbara J. Bina
    Puyallup WA
65   Barbara DuBois
    Socorro NM
66   Robert Chute
    London ON Canada
67   Muriel Rance
    Kimberling City MO
68   Robert Chute
    London ON Canada

69   Brian Smith
    Deux-Montagnes QC Canada
70   Brian Smith
    Deux-Montagnes QC Canada
71   Sandy Fink
    Dowling FL
72   Sheila Forsyth
    Irvington NJ
73   Donald Little
    Salem OH
74   Dennis E. Rager
    Bronx NY
75   Dennis E. Rager
    Bronx NY
76   Dennis E. Rager
    Bronx NY
77   Dennis E. Rager
    Bronx NY
78   Dennis E. Rager
    Bronx NY
79   Brian Smith
    Deux-Montagnes QC Canada
80   Peggy Vermander
    Lexington MI
81   Doris Freeman
    Jackson TN
82   Daniel Elmen
    Lewisville TX
83   Samuel Farahmand
    Woodland Hills CA
84   Ashley Grayson
    Baltimore MD
85   Phyllis J. Neuschwanger
    Platteville CO
86   Lawrence Murphy
    Lincoln NE
87   Judy Muth
    Virginia Beach VA
88   Jerry Wilson
    Mason MI
89   V Pax
    Chicago IL
90   Aaron Patterson
    Rocky River OH
91   Christopher Sorensen
    Rancho Palos Verdes CA
92   Sherwin Kaufman
    New York NY
93   Rod A. Walters
    Rochester NY
94   Ann Robinson
    Sarasota FL
95   Dale Reich
    Oconomowoc WI
96   Linda Aschbrenner
    Marshfield WI
97   Angie Sue Davis
    Weston OH
98   Marie E. Turner
    Laramie WY
99   Jerry Wilson
    Mason MI
100   Graham Kash
    Cookeville TN

STAGE PLAY WINNERS

1. **Carrie Printz**
   Denver CO
2. **Sharilynn La May**
   Summerfield FL
3. **Mervyn Kaufman**
   New York NY
4. **Valerie Stasik**
   Santa Fe NM
5. **Bob Wilson**
   Phoenix AZ
6. **George Taylor**
   Beaverton OR
7. **Charlee Brown**
   Livingston TX
8. **Dean Stewart**
   San Fernando CA
9. **George Taylor**
   Beaverton OR
10. **Jerry Newman**
    Murrieta CA
11. **Jacqueline Little**
    Matthews NC
12. **La'Chris Jordan**
    Seattle WA
13. **Douglas Huff**
    Saint Peter MN
14. **Russell Allen**
    Richmond VA
15. **Christopher Morse**
    Idyllwild CA
16. **Jeffrey Jackson**
    Far Hills NJ
17. **Melanie Faulknor**
    Edmonton AB Canada
18. **Debra Borchert**
    Issaquah WA
19. **Henry Feldman**
    Houston TX
20. **Kathleen McLaughlin**
    La Mesa CA
21. **Leigh Hunt**
    Gig Harbor WA
22. **Lynne Kaufman**
    San Francisco CA
23. **Carrie Printz**
    Denver CO
24. **Robert Lynn**
    Dubuque IA
25. **Alyssa Lord**
    Collegeville PA
26. **James M. Doumas**
    Port Orange FL
27. **Bob Wilson**
    Phoenix AZ
28. **Jewel Seehaus-Fisher**
    Highland Park NJ
29. **Robert Gately**
    Bethlehem PA
30. **Bob Wilson**
    Phoenix AZ
31. **Catherine A. Accardi, Sandra K. Nichols and Constance C. O'Connell**
    Walnut Creek CA
32. **Marilyn Duarte**
    Toronto ON Canada
33. **Doug Baldwin**
    Portland OR
34. **La'Chris Jordan**
    Seattle WA
35. **Don Orwald**
    Granbury TX
36. **Barry Wolcott**
    Bakersfield CA
37. **Robert Gately**
    Bethlehem PA
38. **Carl L. Williams**
    Houston TX
39. **Rory J Thompson**
    West Redding CT
40. **David Allyn**
    Weehawken NJ
41. **Mr. Samuel Ernest Ansah**
    Asare Accra Ghana
42. **Daphne Mintz**
    Norcross GA
43. **Don Orwald**
    Granbury TX
44. **Gina Woodring**
    New Canton VA
45. **Evan Gulford-Blake**
    Stone Mountain GA
46. **Doug Stone**
    Brooklyn NY
47. **Don Orwald**
    Granbury TX
48. **Christopher M. Acosta**
    Marion MS
49. **Kathleen McLaughlin**
    La Mesa CA
50. **Walter Thinnes**
    New York NY
51. **Tanis Galik**
    Tehachapi CA
52. **Carl L. Williams**
    Houston TX
53. **Carlton D Baker II**
    New York NY
54. **James A Marzo**
    Williamsville NY
55. **Nu Quang**
    Seattle WA
56. **Leigh Hunt**
    Gig Harbor WA
57. **Christopher Coey**
    Lexington SC
58. **Pat Renshaw**
    Kerrville TX
59. **Barbara Tylla**
    Racine WI
60. **Sue Ann Culp**
    Zeeland MI
61. **Marcia R Rudin**
    Sanibel FL
62. **S.M.W Hollenbeck**
    Seattle WA
63. **Judith J. Slater**
    Tamarac FL
64. **Sarah Sego**
    Bridgeport CT
65. **Marya Smith**
    Elizabeth IL
66. **Martha Humphreys**
    Huntsville AL
67. **Art Kramer**
    Tucson AZ
68. **Rose-Mary Harrington**
    Ashland OR
69. **Carolyn Bolivar, Ph.D**
    Birmingham AL
70. **Bob Wilson**
    Phoenix AZ
71. **Martin Mannion**
    Belmar NJ
72. **Samantha Drake**
    Berkeley CA
73. **Anne Kern**
    Eugene OR
74. **Don Orwald**
    Granbury TX
75. **Chad Rohrback**
    Chicago IL
76. **Don Orwald**
    Granbury TX
77. **Barrie Kreinik**
    New York NY
78. **Tommacina Bell**
    Katy TX
79. **Joe Molnar**
    Brooklyn NY
80. **Irving Metzman**
    New York NY
81. **Pete Peterson**
    Eugene OR
82. **Louis Standish**
    Astoria NY
83. **Mervyn Kaufman**
    New York NY
84. **Edward Castle**
    Hollywood FL
85. **Augustus M. Cileone**
    Conshohocken PA
86. **Don Orwald**
    Granbury TX
87. **James L. Gossard**
    Ellicott City MD
88. **Don Orwald**
    Granbury TX
89. **Stefanie Steel**
    Brooklyn NY
90. **Dr. Derrick Hurlin**
    Pretoria South Africa
91. **William Gilmore**
    Tampa FL
92. **Yvonne Adalian**
    Vancouver BC Canada
93. **Candy McKinney**
    Sibley MO
94. **MC Johnson**
    DPO AE
95. **Eugene Orlando**
    Seffner FL
96. **Michael L. Job**
    San Francisco CA
97. **Vivian Tolliver**
    Mays Landing NJ
98. **Rilla Angus**
    Everett WA
99. **Kathryn Murdock**
    El Granada CA
100. **Robert Weesner**
    Columbus OH

TELEVISION/MOVIE SCRIPT WINNERS

1 Steve Lowery and Will Swaim
   Irvine CA
2 Tom Lavagnino
   Los Angeles CA
3 Ami McCuaig
   Seattle WA
4 Gail Jenner
   Etna CA
5 Elizabeth Stahl
   San Jose CA
6 Katie Black
   Auburn AL
7 John Jeffire
   Clinton Township MI
8 Gina Leone
   Farmingville NY
9 Sean Fallon
   Montgomery NY
10 Rebecca J. Herring
   Tustin MI
11 Christian White
   Lake Charles LA
12 John Michael Meehan
   Silver Spring MD
13 Paul J. Magliari
   Thornwood NY
14 Christian White
   Lake Charles LA
15 William Gilmore
   Tampa FL
16 Clyde Farnsworth
   Washington DC
17 Shelley Lockwood
   Clarksville TN
18 Robert English
   Huntington Beach CA
19 Michelle L. Chiacchia
   Hamburg NY
20 Carol Ann Lindsay
   Carlsbad CA
21 Heather-Louise Ferris
   Greenwood IL
22 Norman Bradford
   Tucson AZ
23 Heather-Louise Ferris
   Greenwood IL
24 Dale Whisman
   Tulsa OK
25 William Gilmore
   Tampa FL
26 Erik Argenti
   Los Angeles CA
27 Jocelyn Rish
   Summerville SC
28 Sid Smoliga
   West Linn OR
29 Daniel Mullins
   Pleasant Hill OH
30 Lucy A. Fazely
   Oscoda MI
31 John Hart
   Oregon City OR
32 Allie Mire
   Orefield PA
33 Juin Charnell
   St. Paul MN
34 Jennifer Elizabeth
   North Hollywood CA

35 Danielle Greene
   Santa Barbara CA
36 Michael & Andrew Jaworski
   Wonder Lake IL
37 Dale Whisman
   Tulsa OK
38 Dean Stewart
   Sylmar CA
39 John Michael Meehan
   Silver Spring MD
40 Kyle Michel Sullivan
41 Dean Stewart
   Sylmar CA
42 Payton Kane
   Highland Heights KY
43 Hillel F. Damron
   Sacramento CA
44 Dan Tomasulo
   Sea Girt NJ
45 Sam Cromartie
   Ormond Beach FL
46 Jakki Clarke Fletcher
   Merchantville NJ
47 Debra Cutshaw
   Gardnerville NV
48 Tom Swinson
   Park Rapids MN
49 Marguerite Ashton
   Fort Atkinson WI
50 Justin and April Pollack
   Jamestown ND
51 Robert Brandon Henderson
   Missoula MT
52 Jason Lohr
   Montrose CA
53 Heather Mulvany
   Rineyville KY
54 Daryl Malarry Davidson
   Athens OH
55 Sam Buttari
   Bloomfield NJ
56 Lisa Bastian
   Temecula CA
57 Susan Traxel
   Dodge ND
58 Kimberly Kaplan
   La Crescenta CA
59 Sandra Jackson-Opoku
   Chicago IL
60 Silvia L. Gomez
   East Portland OR
61 Stephen Gary Politowicz
   Los Angeles CA
62 Sid Smoliga
   West Linn OR
63 Timothy P. Remp
   Hudson NH
64 Irving Metzman
   New York NY
65 Howard Risk
   Eagle CO
66 Catherine M. Cummings
   Beverly Hills CA
67 Leland Little
   Anchorage AK
68 Kevin Given and Chris Geary
   Los Angeles CA

69 Stephanie Olivieri
   Burbank CA
70 Dana Booker and Ralph Brem
   Cleveland OH
71 Ron Iannone
   Morgantown WV
72 Rick Demille Little
   Elm TX
73 Sid Smoliga
   West Linn OR
74 Lonnie Bradley
   Salt Lake City UT
75 Sean Fallon
   Montgomery NY
76 Ronald Petty
   Orland CA
77 David M. Thomas
   Monterey CA
78 Daniel Moriarty
   Reynoldsburg OH
79 John Wood
   Las Vegas NV
80 Terry Ward Tucker
   Folly Beach SC
81 Barbara Gengler
   Pittsburgh PA
82 Michelle L. Chiacchia
   Hamburg NY
83 Ann Paris
   Massillon OH
84 C. V. Herst
   Oakland CA
85 Sadena Corbin
   Jacksonville NC
86 Cora Kerr
   El Cajon CA
87 Jenniffer Castillo
   Manhattan Beach CA
88 Peggy Bray
   Carlsbad CA
89 Robert Negron
   New York NY
90 Alec Sias
   Kingwood TX
91 La Juana Y. Green
   New York NY
92 Victoria Zakrzewski
   Meriden CT
93 Sid Smoliga
   West Linn OR
94 Walter Stafford
   Macon GA
95 James Karantonis
   Columbia MD
96 Stephen Schwandt
   Naples FL
97 Daniel Mullins
   Pleasant Hill OH
98 Mike Perry
   Kippens NL Canada
99 Kelly A. Swan
   Londonderry NH
100 Lydia Richardson
   Columbus OH